Neuroaesthetics and the Art of Transformation

Through an imaginative engagement with neuroaesthetics, this vividly illustrated book presents the imagery of the forest as a creative metaphor for reenvisioning the structures of the brain, distressing mental health conditions such as anxiety and obsessive-compulsive disorder (OCD), the potential for transformation, and the process of finding a new pathway forward.

The book offers a highly innovative and accessible framework for approaching basic neuroanatomy and related mental processes. The metaphorical imagery of deer trails through the woods provides a suggestive means to visualize what it might look like if a person could see inside their own brain when they are peaceful and content, and to view the pathways that form through the repetition of their thought patterns. This would be like having a window into the inner world of the mind and the brain. Within the human nervous system, neurons are nerve cells that transmit information, and all thoughts leave a neuronal trail. Both the trails *and* the information that passes through them provide the building blocks of a neuroaesthetic fairytale. Divided into three parts, the book examines the structural similarities between the forest and the brain, tells a story about getting lost in the woods and finding your way back again, and then builds on resonant themes of growth, transformation, and finding a new path forward.

Featuring exercises including imaginative visualizations, reflective journaling questions, and creative writing prompts, this book will be a useful supplement to those already practicing and those studying to be expressive arts therapists, educators, therapists, counsellors, social workers, and psychologists, as well as people who wish to utilize this material for their own journey.

This book builds on the insights and aesthetic approach featured in the author's previous books *The Colors of Life: Exploring Life Experience Through Color and Emotion* and *Approaching SEL Through Emotion and Color with Advanced Learners: A Companion to the Colors of Life.*

Marcia Brennan, PhD is a career educator and an award-winning teacher and author. She is the Carolyn and Fred McManis Professor of Humanities at Rice University in Houston, Texas, USA, where she also serves as professor of both art history and religious studies. Since 2009, she has also served as Artist in Residence in the Department of Palliative, Rehabilitation, and Integrative Medicine at the University of Texas M.D. Anderson Cancer Center. In 2021, she expanded this practice to serve as Literary Artist at the hospital of the University of Pennsylvania, where she works in both general oncology and transplantation oncology. She is the recipient of the Georgia O'Keeffe Museum Research Center Book Prize, the Steve Thorney Award for the Promotion of Humanitarian and Spiritual Care in the Clinical Field, and Rice University's George R. Brown Award for Superior Teaching.

Neuroaesthetics and the Art of Transformation

Deer Trails Through the Woods

Marcia Brennan

Routledge
Taylor & Francis Group

NEW YORK AND LONDON

Designed cover image: Hannah Li, Deer Trails Through the Woods, 2024

First published 2026
by Routledge
605 Third Avenue, New York, NY 10158

and by Routledge
4 Park Square, Milton Park, Abingdon, Oxon, OX14 4RN

Routledge is an imprint of the Taylor & Francis Group, an informa business

© 2026 Marcia Brennan

ISBN: 978-1-041-04076-7 (hbk)
ISBN: 978-1-041-04073-6 (pbk)
ISBN: 978-1-003-62672-5 (ebk)

DOI: 10.4324/9781003626725

Typeset in Times New Roman
by Apex CoVantage, LLC

For Amanda
and for Raphael

Contents

About the Author and Illustrators

Marcia Brennan, PhD is a career educator and an award-winning teacher and author. She is the Carolyn and Fred McManis Professor of Humanities at Rice University in Houston, Texas, where she also serves as Professor of both Art History and Religious Studies. She is the author of 13 scholarly monographs and exhibition catalogues. Her book *Painting Gender, Constructing Theory: The Alfred Stieglitz Circle and American Formalist Aesthetics* (MIT Press) was awarded the Georgia O'Keeffe Museum Research Center Book Prize. Among her numerous art historical volumes, she is the co-author of *Modern Mystic: The Art of Hyman Bloom* (Distributed Art Publishers), which was produced in conjunction with a major retrospective exhibition at the Boston Museum of Fine Arts. In the field of Education, she is the author of *The Colors of Life: Exploring Life Experience Through Color and Emotion* (Routledge) and *Approaching SEL Through Emotion and Color with Advanced Learners: A Companion to the Colors of Life* (Routledge). She has also developed complementary research areas in literary aesthetics and psychosocial oncology. Since 2009, she has served as Artist in Residence in the Department of Palliative, Rehabilitation, and Integrative Medicine at the University of Texas M.D.

Anderson Cancer Center. In 2021, she expanded this practice to serve as Literary Artist at the Hospital of the University of Pennsylvania, where she works in both General Oncology and Transplantation Oncology. In 2025, M.D. Anderson honored her with the Steve Thorney Award for the Promotion of Humanitarian and Spiritual Care in the Clinical Field. Her clinical work has resulted in the publication of three volumes, the most recent of which is *A Rose from Two Gardens: Saint Thérèse of Lisieux and Images of the End of Life* (University of California Medical Humanities Press). She is the recipient of fellowships from the American Council of Learned Societies and the Samuel H. Kress Foundation. Throughout her career, she has been honored with 14 awards or recognitions for her teaching, including being selected four times as the recipient of Rice University's George R. Brown Award for Superior Teaching.

Hannah Li is a biomedical researcher at the National Institutes of Health, where she studies the genetic basis of Type 2 diabetes. She graduated from Rice University in 2024 with a degree in Biosciences. As a lifelong illustrator and painter, Hannah enjoys using art to make complex emotional and scientific ideas more approachable for young audiences. She hopes to combine research, medicine, and creativity in a future career as a physician-scientist.

Madison Zhao is a freelance artist based in Bethesda, Maryland. She earned a BA in Neuroscience with a minor in Medical Humanities from Rice University, and she is passionate about blending art with medicine to foster empathy in healthcare. As an aspiring physician, she is particularly interested in creating visual narratives and working on projects ranging from medical diagrams to picture book illustrations.

Acknowledgments

One book emerged as I was writing another. Sometimes it happens that way. As I was writing *The Colors of Life: Exploring Life Experience Through Color and Emotion,* I did a substantial amount of research relating to the youth mental health crisis. This material ultimately found its way into an accompanying book for parents and educators, *Approaching Emotion and Color Through SEL with Advanced Learners.* While writing these books, I came to see that challenging mental health issues can arise not only among young people, but also among people of all ages. As I dove into the bibliography on neuroanatomy, I was struck by the sheer number of terms relating to the natural landscape. Given that I had just spent the past two years writing a book on color and emotion, a creative framework began to emerge, which ultimately crystallized into a neurocognitive fairytale.

Such an exploration would never have been possible without the support and guidance of many people. Foremost among them is Amanda Hohlstein. As was the case with *The Colors of Life,* Amanda was there through every stage and phase of the project. She is an amazing collaborative presence and a source of remarkable wisdom and insight, generosity and grace.

As was also the case with *The Colors of Life* books, I again had the great privilege of working with Hannah Li and

Madison Zhao as both research assistants and illustrators. They were the first people to hear about the concept of deer trails through the woods as a metaphorical framework for neurocognitive exploration. From the tenderest point in the journey, they were extremely supportive and encouraging, asking excellent questions, offering valuable suggestions, and creating amazing images. Even when this book was still just the spark of an idea glimmering on a storyboard, Hannah and Madison were always willing to see where the pathways led. I am also grateful for the feedback provided by my Rice students, especially Maria Hancu, Ioana Murgulet, Daniel Wang, and Leo Zhang. It is an extraordinary privilege to work with such wonderful students and to have such rich opportunities for learning and exchange.

Another former student, Dr. Rishab Ramapriyan, kindly read an extended version of the entire book proposal and offered invaluable comments while preparing to undertake his Residency in Neurosurgery. Nathan Carlin's wisdom and insights similarly shaped this project at an intrinsic level. Elisabeth Papadopoulos has been a continual source of encouragement and inspiration as I have constructed imaginative worlds. From a different perspective, that of a career educator and school leader, Neil Holt offered valuable reflections on the importance of neuroscience within secondary education. I am also extremely grateful to my colleagues and friends, both within and beyond Rice University, especially Judith Brunton, Jose Chapa, Anne Klein, Brian Ogren, N.J. Pierce, and Lane Transou.

This project was supported by the Office of the Dean of the School of Humanities, and Christy Montecillo has my

heartfelt thanks. Adriana Campos Chiaramonti provided
expert administrative assistance and support throughout
all stages of this work, and I am beyond grateful to her.
This project was also supported by Rice University's
Medical Humanities Research Institute. I am grateful to the
Institute's Director Kirsten Ostherr and to the Executive
Administrator Tiffany Morgan for their kindness, support,
and encouragement.

At Routledge, my editors Ellie Broadhurst and Hannah
Rich have been amazingly wise, generous, and supportive.
They have my deepest thanks, as do Aakriti Aggarwal,
Pramoth Jaikishan, Kamali Samynathan, and Pragati
Sharma. My gratitude also goes to the anonymous peer
review readers who offered valuable suggestions on this
project.

This book contains several stories that are drawn directly
from my clinical work with people at the end of life and
with those who are actively fighting for their life with
aggressive cancer. I am so grateful to everyone who
generously shared their story, and to my colleagues at
both the M.D. Anderson Cancer Center and the Hospital
of the University of Pennsylvania, especially Dr. Eduardo
Bruera and Dr. Ahsan Azhar. I would also like to thank
Chanelle Clerc, Michelle Feil, Michael Guzzardi, Eletta
Kershaw, Joanne Klein, Thuc Nguyen, Ylaine Ong-Gabat,
and Stephanie Rossi. Dr. Jennifer Wheler is the founder
of the nonprofit organization COLLAGE: ART FOR
CANCER, which facilitates my hospital work. This clinical

work would not have been possible without Dr. Wheler's extraordinary vision and initiative.

Themes relating to Chapter 24 first appeared in the *HYPERLINK "https://online.fliphtml5.com/xirjy/uszf/" \t "_blank"Boletín de Humanidades Médicas* 18 (Tucumán, Argentina: Laboratorio di Humanidades Médicas, 2024). I would like to thank the journal's editor Dr. Francisco Juan José Viola for his kind invitation to contribute to this volume and to reproduce aspects of the discussion here.

I would also like to thank my family, especially my sister Camille Gagliardi, her wife Dana Gillette, my cousin Alison Healey, and my husband Scott Brennan. As always, your love and support mean the world.

Not least of all, I would like to thank everyone who reads this book and takes the time to explore the challenging issues that it raises. This book is for you.

Note Regarding Issues of Confidentiality

In compliance with the federal standards of the US Health Insurance Portability and Accountability Act (HIPAA), within this volume particular details relating to specific individuals have been altered or generalized so as to omit any identifiable data. These precautions are consistent with HIPAA compliance while preserving issues of confidentiality, particularly as specified under "The Privacy Rule", The Belmont Report, and the Department of Health and Human Services Office for Human Research Protections, including The Common Rule and subparts B, C, and D of the Health and Human Service specifications as outlined in the Code of Federal Regulations (CFR) at 45 CFR 164 and 165, which specifies the "safe harbor" method of de-identification. By adopting this approach, the stories are presented in such a way as to make the subjects visible *and* to acknowledge the legal and ethical frameworks that make such representations possible at all. Thus, while the descriptions of encounters with patients and caregivers accurately reflect the nature of our interactions, and while the italicized texts are transcriptions of people's statements, these elements are generically worded, thus rendering the subjects anonymous.

This work has been favorably reviewed by two independent Institutional Review Boards (IRBs) at Rice University and at the M.D. Anderson Cancer Center.

Part I: The Brain and the Forest

A Neurocognitive Fairytale

Chapter 1: Deer Trails Through the Woods

Finding a New Path Forward

This is a magical book about brains and forests, thought and language.

Figure 1.1

DOI: 10.4324/9781003626725-2

Have you ever seen a deer trail through the woods?
If you were walking,
And you were to come up above the woods,
Up above the forest,
You would see many wonderful, beautiful, natural trails
Made by the animals whose tracks are interlinking,
Intertwining,
Taking them to all their natural resources,
To places they need to go,
For rest,
For food,
For water,
For community.
This would all be in a lush green forest,
With deep brown earth,
And wherever you turn,
Wherever you look,
The pathways are very beautiful.

The Metaphorical Imagery of Deer Trails Through the Woods

Much like the pathways of a natural landscape, the structures of the human brain generally look the same for everyone, even as the individual experiences, histories, and stories that unfold in these spaces are unique for each person. The metaphorical imagery of deer trails through the woods provides a suggestive way to visualize what it might look like if a person could see inside their own brain when they are peaceful and content, and to view the pathways that form through the repetition of their thought patterns.

This would be like having a window into the inner world of the mind and the brain.

When I first started doing the research for this book, I was struck by the sheer number of terms within descriptive neuroanatomy that related to the natural landscape.[1] As I reflected on this vocabulary, the metaphor of the forest—and then of deer trails through the woods—began to emerge. As you engage with these metaphors, you may start to picture a living landscape in your own mind, as well.

Within the human nervous system, neurons are nerve cells that both receive and transmit information, and all thoughts leave a neuronal trail. Both the trails and the information that passes through them provide the building blocks of a neurocognitive fairytale. In this context, the word "neurocognitive" is especially resonant. The prefix "neuro" refers to nerves and to the nervous system, while the root, "cognition", means "knowing together".[2] As you will see, many different types of knowledge come together through the metaphorical imagery of deer trails through the woods.[3]

Sometimes walking through life can feel a bit like walking through a maze that is filled with twists and turns, vines and brambles. This book can show you how to get out of a labyrinth of difficult thinking, and how to replace old patterns with new ones. The book is divided into three parts. The first part examines the structural similarities between the forest and the brain. The second part tells a story about getting lost in the woods and finding your way back again. This section is filled with suggestive metaphors for visualizing anxiety and obsessive-compulsive disorder (OCD). The third part builds on resonant themes of growth, transformation, and finding a new path forward.

These subjects are approached through the lens of neuroaesthetics. The field of neuroaesthetics examines how the brain responds to creative stimuli, including the production and contemplation of works of art.[4] This book both mirrors and extends the familiar methodological approaches associated with neuroaesthetics. It examines how the structures of the human brain, and its related patterns of thought, can form the bases of an innovative conceptual artwork that can help to shape a person's thinking.[5] Thus, rather than primarily studying the effects of aesthetics in and on the human brain, the book draws on analytical frameworks within descriptive neuroaesthetics—particularly visual metaphors and analogical thinking—to reimagine the psychic landscape itself.

Research has shown that when people engage with visual metaphors and creative analogies, the limbic system is activated to trigger a reward response in the brain. People feel a sense of pleasure when they recognize the similarities between otherwise dissimilar subjects, such as the resonance between neuronal pathways and deer trails through the woods.[6] Scientific inquiries relating to the mapping of the brain represent a growing area of interest in our culture. Research into how the brain works, and what it needs to thrive and survive, is increasing exponentially. This area of exploration is—and it will be—the focus of much science, much art, much thinking, and much philosophy in the years to come.

Seeing Both the Forest and the Trees

How do we begin to see subjects that are so subtle and
complex that they are often difficult to see? We can
practice by holding multiple perspectives at once. You've
all heard the saying: "A person can't see the forest for the
trees". This expression means that a person gets so bogged
down in the details of life that they can't see the bigger
picture. There are times when we need to look closely at
individual details that may seem small and insignificant,
but which can hold worlds of meaning. And then there are
times when we need to step back to see the larger patterns
that emerge. This book can help you practice the art of
holding such multiple perspectives at once.

One way to undertake this type of exploration is to look
carefully at both the detailed ink drawings and the loose
watercolor paintings appearing throughout this volume.
Notice the stylistic differences between the soft watercolor
landscape at the beginning of this chapter and the crisp
linear illustrations appearing in the next one. In the
opening chapter, the forest displays many interlinking
pathways and many layers of presence. The tonal keynotes
of the painting include grounded shades of rich brown
and deep emerald green. In this scene, a curving pathway
is flanked by a deer, a red fox, some squirrels, and the
various tracks that these woodland creatures make. The
underlying ink drawing provides a stable framework to
support the overlying layers of loose watercolor washes.
Much as in life itself, in this scene an entire world comes
into being through multiple layers of presence. Consciously
observing the relations between the individual details and

the larger patterns that emerge is an example of the art of "knowing together"—or, of cognition.

Exercise for Reflection and Journaling

Each chapter is followed by exercises for journaling and reflection, including imaginative visualizations and creative writing prompts. When you do the exercises at the end of each chapter, you are using this as a workbook to help shape your own growth and learning processes. You are also cultivating your own neural malleability, while anchoring the insights and making them uniquely your own.

As you read, record your observations and responses in a journal. Always date your journal entries and make special note of any insights that arise, including any significant shifts in your thinking. The journal can provide an important record of your progress. Recording and analyzing your insights can increase your levels of self-awareness and detachment, qualities that can help you to better manage your responses to various situations. As one of my students put it:

> The very act of portraying my personal experiences in words places me, the narrator, as a detached third-person observer. Reading the narrative sequence through the lens of the detached observer is a grounding experience that allows me to make balanced judgements on my intuitive emotional responses to the scenario. As the narrator, the language that I choose in creating a story indicates where my gaze is focused, what my attention falls on, and where my mind wanders. This type of observation [lets me be] both attached and detached at the same time.

Throughout this book, I encourage readers to practice, practice, and practice the exercises that follow each chapter. When you build a new muscle, you can always use that muscle in times of stress. Yet it is much better not to wait until you are actually in distress to begin building the muscle. Once you've practiced connecting to new ways of thinking, then you've already created the relationships inside of yourself, and you can use the skills more quickly and effectively, no matter what circumstances arise.

Neuroaesthetics and the Art of Transformation is filled with metaphors relating to nature. If there is a place in nature that you particularly like, you can always practice sitting there and tuning into the feelings that arise in your mind and body. If you love animals, you can also practice consciously tuning into the feelings that you have when you're connecting with a special animal. Make careful note of the feelings that emerge, and practice anchoring those feelings in your mind and body. Then, in a moment of stress, the connection is already so strong that it's readily available and much easier to access.

Please also keep in mind that journals are private spaces that can be kept to oneself or shared selectively because your writings are reflections of your own mind and heart.

Notes

1 These terms include dendrites, pathways, arborizations, limbs, ridges, stalks, briars, brambles, climbing fibers, mosses, spines (or "spinules"), thorns (or "thorny excrescences"), and brush (including "brush cells"

and "brush synapses"). See, for example, Ronald S.
Petralia et al., "Structure, Distribution, and Function of
Neuronal/Synaptic Spinules and Related Invaginating
Projections", *Neuromolecular Medicine* 17, no. 3
(September 2015): https://www.ncbi.nlm.nih.gov/pmc/
articles/PMC4536166/

2 The prefix *co* means with or together, while the root
   (g)nōscĕre indicates both knowledge and the process
   of knowing something consciously. See the entry on
   "cognition" in the *Oxford English Dictionary*, 2nd ed.
   (Oxford: Clarendon Press, 1989): https://www.oed.com/
   dictionary/cognition_n?tab=meaning_and_use#9078506
   Hereafter, references will be to the *OED*.

3 Within the field of Education, neuroscience relates to
   key issues concerning patterns of learning, emotional
   processing, cognitive ability, and problem-solving
   skills. As Glenn Whitman and Ian Kelleher have
   observed: "There is no greater opportunity to achieve
   [a quality education] than in integrating research from
   education, behavioral psychology, and cognitive science
   into the daily work of teachers and the thinking of
   school leaders". See Glenn Whitman and Ian Kelleher,
   NeuroTeach: Brain Science and the Future of Education
   (Lanham, MD: Rowman & Littlefield, 2016), 5. As
   the authors note, such an approach allows teaching
   to be approached as both an art and a science. For
   a discussion of practical applications of educational
   neuroscience in the classroom, including how the brain
   changes through applied experiences and structured
   learning activities, see Bruce McCandliss and Elizabeth
   Toomarian, "Putting Neuroscience in the Classroom:

How the Brain Changes as We Learn", *Trend Magazine* (April 13, 2020): https://www.pewtrusts.org/en/trend/archive/spring-2020/putting-neuroscience-in-the-classroom-how-the-brain-changes-as-we-learn

4 For a discussion of neuroaesthetics in the classroom, see Faith A. Pak and Ethan B. Reichsman, "Beauty and the Brain: The Emerging Field of Neuroaesthetics", *The Harvard Crimson* (November 10, 2017): https://www.thecrimson.com/article/2017/11/10/neuroaesthetics-cover/

For a reference work that summarizes key themes in this emerging field, see Martin Skov and Marcus Nadal, eds., *The Routledge International Handbook of Neuroaesthetics* (New York: Routledge, 2023). This volume focuses on issues relating to aesthetic preference and to the corresponding responses within artistic experience.

5 In *The Aesthetic Brain: How We Evolved to Desire Beauty and Enjoy Art* (New York: Oxford University Press, 2014), the neuroscientist Anjan Chatterjee identifies important connections between aesthetics, neuroscience, and evolutionary biology. Chatterjee notes that "the evidence from brain studies shows that there is no specific neural network dedicated to aesthetics" (p. xxii), including artistic sensations, emotions, or meanings. Instead, aesthetic responses involve a complex modular enterprise within the brain.

6 For foundational work on these subjects, see V.S. Ramachandran and William Hirstein, "The Science of Art: A Neurological Theory of Aesthetic Experience", *Journal of Consciousness Studies* 6, no. 6–7 (1999): 15–51: https://web.archive.org/web/20120302011954/http://www.imprint.co.uk/rama/art.pdf

References

Chatterjee, Anjan. *The Aesthetic Brain: How We Evolved to Desire Beauty and Enjoy Art*. New York: Oxford University Press. 2014.

McCandliss, Bruce, and Elizabeth Toomarian. "Putting Neuroscience in the Classroom: How the Brain Changes as We Learn." *Trend Magazine*, April 13, 2020. https://www.pewtrusts.org/en/trend/archive/spring-2020/putting-neuroscience-in-the-classroom-how-the-brain-changes-as-we-learn

Pak, Faith A., and Ethan B. Reichsman. "Beauty and the Brain: The Emerging Field of Neuroaesthetics." *The Harvard Crimson,* November 10, 2017. https://www.thecrimson.com/article/2017/11/10/neuroaesthetics-cover/

Petralia, Ronald S., Ya-Xian Wang, Mark P. Mattson, and Pamela J. Yao. "Structure, Distribution, and Function of Neuronal/Synaptic Spinules and Related Invaginating Projections." *Neuromolecular Medicine* 17, no. 3 (September 2015). https://www.ncbi.nlm.nih.gov/pmc/articles/PMC4536166/

Ramachandran, V.S., and William Hirstein. "The Science of Art: A Neurological Theory of Aesthetic Experience." *Journal of Consciousness Studies* 6, no. 6–7 (1999): 15–51. https://web.archive.org/web/20120302011954/http://www.imprint.co.uk/rama/art.pdf

Simpson, J.A., and E.S.C. Weiner, eds. *The Oxford English Dictionary*. 2nd ed. Oxford: Clarendon Press. 1989.

Skov, Martin, and Marcus Nadal, eds. *The Routledge International Handbook of Neuroaesthetics*. New York: Routledge. 2023.

Whitman, Glenn, and Ian Kelleher. *Neuroteach: Brain Science and the Future of Education*. Lanham, MD: Rowman & Littlefield. 2016.

Chapter 2: This Book Is a Gift

Who This Book Is For

Some people get a gift and they don't open it. Other people get a gift, they open it, and they throw it away. Still others get a gift, they open it, and they cherish it.

Figure 2.1

DOI: 10.4324/9781003626725-3

This book is a gift. You can open it, love it, wear it, sleep in it, and it can become your favorite thing. Or, you can throw it away. Whatever you choose is up to you.

This Book Is for Everyone

This book is written for the general public, as well as for students, teachers, and clinicians. Some readers will be drawn to this book because they are fascinated by the workings of the human brain and its potential for creative expression. Others may be experiencing anxiety or obsessive-compulsive disorder (OCD) in their own life, or in the life of someone close to them, and they may be hungry for a solution. For those readers, this book can provide a sense of accompaniment. One thing that people with anxiety and OCD tend *not* to do is to seek help until there is quite a bind. When a person looks at the images or reads the poems in this book, they can always take a deep breath and reset themselves moment by moment, feeling by feeling, breath by breath. This book features many short chapters that intersperse scientific information with poetry and paintings in ways that create breathing space for the reader.

Because I work with both college students and hospital patients, I see that there is a clear and growing need for such a book within our social, educational, and clinical contexts. As our understanding of neuroscience and neuroaesthetics continues to grow, so too does the potential to apply this knowledge to enhance our everyday life experience. The book's short chapters and vivid, engaging imagery will appeal to independent readers, as well as to busy clinicians who may wish to recommend the book to their patients. If you really like this book, you can always consider giving a copy to your therapist and saying, "You read this, and we'll do the work together".

Neuroaesthetics and the Art of Transformation is written for students at all levels, especially for people in their late teens and early twenties who are interested in studying neuroaesthetics, psychology, mental health, anxiety, trauma, and OCD.[1] The book is not only written for those who are experiencing these conditions in their own life, or in the life of someone they know, but it is also aimed at educating those who are studying to be psychologists, social workers, counsellors, educators, translational scientists, creative artists, and expressive arts therapists. It can show these readers how to incorporate a language of accessibility and creativity when engaging with people their own age and younger.

By the time a person is diagnosed with severe anxiety or OCD, they are usually in their late teens or early twenties. Before then, such distressing behavior patterns may be considered a quaint personality trait and something that a young person will eventually grow out of. OCD is rarely diagnosed until the condition anchors in more deeply, and there is the courage to give such a diagnosis. By the time a person is in their late teens and early twenties, severe anxiety and OCD may already be creating an upheaval in the person's life and in the lives of those around them. If the condition is not caught early, it can follow a person around for a long time and sometimes it can create quite a nightmare. For readers who want to do the work, this book can help teach the art of transformation.

Ribbons of Dendrites

Books are symbols of knowledge, and there is something special about the book that appears at the beginning of this chapter. If you look closely, you will see that the book is wrapped in a green ribbon tied up in a bow—yet the ribbon is made of strands of dendrites. Dendrites are the branching forms found in tree limbs and tree roots. Dendrites are also the branching fibers found in neurons or in the nerve cells of the brain. According to the *Oxford English Dictionary* (or *OED*, for short), dendrites appear in nature as "a crystalline growth of branching or arborescent form". They are also "any of one or more processes from a nerve cell which are typically short and extensively branched and which conduct impulses toward the cell body".[2]

Not only is the book wrapped in a ribbon of dendrites, but it is also surrounded by flashing golden sparkles. Just as the sparks appear to be decorative and magical, they evoke the energetic flashes of neuronal firing. As you read these words, perhaps you can picture your own neurons flashing as new ideas light up your mind like the golden sparkles surrounding the book. Why does this happen? Why do the sparks fly when we read? As human beings, we love language. Everyone loves a good story. Our stories are full of symbols and rich in metaphors, such as the imagery of deer trails through the woods, or a book wrapped up in a ribbon of dendrites.

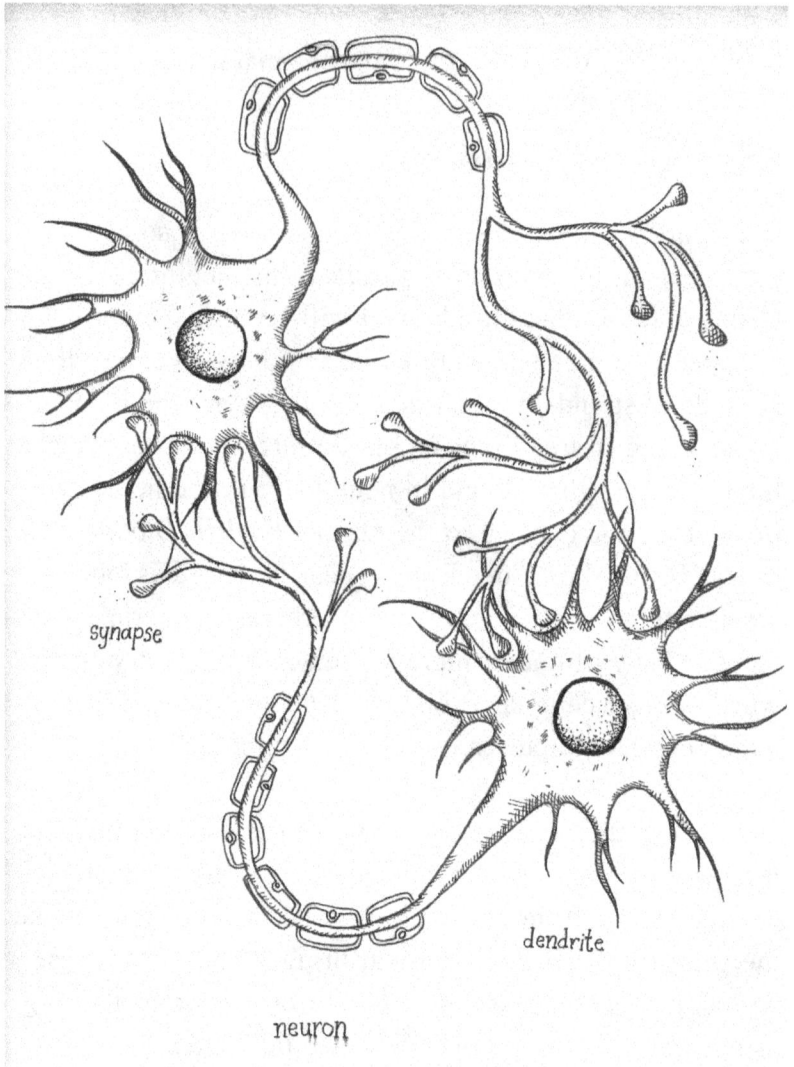

synapse

dendrite

neuron

Figure 2.2

This book is a gift because it can help you to look deeply within yourself, within your own mind and brain. Turning your gaze inward creates a sense of conscious awareness. Such knowledge can shed important light on the power of your own intelligence, your own creativity, your own learning style, and your own capacity to make choices. This knowledge can help you to see and do things differently, if you wish.

These are just some of the ways in which this book is a gift. It's all up to you what you choose to do with it. For those who want to keep reading, the pathways lead to a magical classroom, where I'm waiting to greet you. . . .

Exercise for Reflection and Journaling

This exercise introduces the art of quieting the mind so that you can be more present to yourself. This exercise also allows you to consciously observe how you are feeling, and to find descriptive language for your subtle states of consciousness.

Please complete the following sentences in your journal:

> This is how I feel right now . . .
> I would describe my state of mind as . . .

There are no "right" or "wrong" answers to these questions. Just be thoughtful and honest with yourself as you note your feelings. Once you have done this, read the opening poem in the previous chapter silently, to yourself.

Allow yourself to see and feel the creative imagery of the deer trails through the woods. Then go back and complete the following sentences:

After reading the poem, this is how I feel now . . .
I would now describe my state of mind as . . .

Now, read the poem aloud. Pay close attention to the metaphorical imagery, and to the cadence of the lines. Be conscious of the places where your own breath rises and falls naturally as you read the words aloud. You can even read the poem twice, if you like. Then look closely at the watercolor painting. Go back to your journal and note:

Now that I've read the poem aloud and I've looked carefully at the painting, this is how I feel . . .
I would describe my state of mind as . . .

Make special note of any shifts in your thinking. You may feel differently, or you may not. The important thing is to find language to express how you are feeling so that you can consciously recognize your own state of mind and how you respond to creative words and images. If you are calm and peaceful throughout this exercise, then you have a good baseline for recognizing your own relaxed state of mind. If you are feeling any strong emotions before you read, then you have an opportunity to evaluate whether reading the poem and looking at the accompanying imagery can help to shift you to a calmer, more peaceful state of mind.

Part of the gift of this exercise is that if you experienced a sense of uplift or calm, peace or joy, as you read the poem or looked at the watercolor, then you know that you can always go back and read the words and look at the picture again, and you can see if they inspire the same feelings. By making conscious note of your own state of mind, you are practicing the fine art of being present to yourself. You are also learning how to be an artist who works in the medium of language and human consciousness. And how *amazing* is that?

Notes

1 I have written a related book on the creative possibilities associated with color, emotion, and experience: *The Colors of Life: Exploring Life Experience Through Color and Emotion* (New York: Routledge, 2025). The companion guide is entitled *Approaching SEL Through Emotion and Color with Advanced Learners: A Companion to the Colors of Life* (New York: Routledge, 2025). While aimed at a younger readership, these books represent part of a larger exploration relating to issues of mental health, education, aesthetics, and self-care.
2 See the entry on "dendrite" in the *OED*: https://www. oed.com/dictionary/dendrite_n?tab=meaning_and_use #7113323

References

Brennan, Marcia. *Approaching SEL Through Emotion and Color with Advanced Learners: A Companion to The Colors of Life*. New York: Routledge. 2025.

Brennan, Marcia. *The Colors of Life: Exploring Life Experience Through Color and Emotion.* New York: Routledge. 2025.

Simpson, J.A., and E.S.C. Weiner, eds. *The Oxford English Dictionary.* 2nd ed. Oxford: Clarendon Press. 1989.

Chapter 3: The Magical Classroom

The Superpowers of Observation and Description

Please come in!

Figure 3.1

DOI: 10.4324/9781003626725-4

My name is Marcia Brennan, and I am a real professor, even though you see me sitting here in an imaginary classroom that lives inside this book. At the outset, let me tell you a bit about this project.

By training, I am not a neuroscientist or a psychiatrist. Nor am I a therapist or an art therapist.[1] I am a professor of the Humanities at a research university, where both my scholarship and my teaching engage the fields of modern and contemporary art history, the medical humanities, and the philosophy of religion. Since early 2009, I have also served as Artist in Residence in the Department of Palliative, Rehabilitation, and Integrative Medicine at the University of Texas M.D. Anderson Cancer Center. In early 2021, I expanded this practice to serve as a literary artist in the fields of general oncology and transplantation oncology at the Hospital of the University of Pennsylvania.[2]

Just as my work bridges many different domains of knowledge, I adopt a hybrid approach throughout *Neuroaesthetics and the Art of Transformation*. In this book, I summarize the scholarly literature on neuroaesthetics and neuroscience for a general reader, and I present related concepts through the lenses of the arts and humanities. Too often in our culture, the sciences, the arts, and the humanities are pitted against one another rather than being seen as complementary pathways of knowledge. The field of neuroaesthetics draws these domains together in novel ways. As one researcher has observed: "It may not even be possible to extricate humanities research from science research when studying aesthetic experience".[3] The creative storytelling methods featured in this book promote various forms of interdisciplinary learning, while helping readers to tap into less conscious and highly evocative aspects of their own mind.

The Imaginary Classroom

With these themes in mind, let's take a closer look at the imaginary classroom. As you can see, this room is filled with intriguing objects. On the table behind me, you see a model of the human brain. Some basic knowledge of neuroanatomy is foundational for the explorations that follow. On the wall in front of me, you see colorful scans of the human brain. These PET (positron emission tomography) scans allow researchers to see inside a living body and to observe how the organs function. We'll be looking more closely at these scans in Part II of the book.

On the shelves behind me, you see some books and a microscope, all of which are tools of vision and knowledge. Microscopic views of a subject allow you to see things that you couldn't see otherwise and to make connections between seemingly dissimilar subjects. Beneath the microscope there is an English Brown Betty teapot, which is there because I collect this particular type of teapot, and I always have a cup of tea close at hand whenever I write or teach (just ask my students). Opposite the teapot is a crystalline rock, while an image of a giant snowflake hangs above the model of the brain. In the third section of the book, we'll examine how these objects exhibit complementary dendritic structures that resonate with both plant life and the brain. On the windowsill, you see some potted philodendrons. The name of this plant means a "love of trees" (*philo* + *dendron*). Taken together, these items shed light on the interconnectedness of the world and various pathways of knowledge.

The Superpowers of Observation and Description

When you undertake this type of exploration, it is important to know your own mind very well. Practicing the skills of observation and description can help you to recognize your own patterns of thinking and your own styles of learning and expression. One way to approach these subjects is to adopt the perspective of the "impartial spectator". This concept was formulated by the eighteenth-century Scottish philosopher and political economist Adam Smith. In *The Theory of Moral Sentiments* (1759), Smith observed that an inner presence resides within each person. This presence is always there and it witnesses everything with a detached perspective, including one's own behaviors, thoughts, and emotions.[4]

The concept of detachment is important on many levels. The basic idea is to see life with great clarity and to not be overly attached to whatever you are looking at or thinking at any given moment. Thoughts are transient, and a person's emotions are constantly shifting. Yet there is a part of you that lies beyond the shifting currents of your thoughts and feelings. Think about it this way: Sometimes you're happy, and sometimes you're sad. Either way, you still exist. All thoughts and emotions come and go. But there is a part of you that is constant, and it can always be relied upon.

Practicing the art of detached observation can give you a greater sense of freedom. This is especially important if there are aspects of your life that you want to change. As you practice seeing the world from multiple perspectives at once, you can experiment with the different possibilities that arise. As you do this, it's like you're running your own little scientific experiments. Becoming a detached observer can help you to stay with the experiments longer, to recognize significant shifts in your thinking, and to make necessary adjustments as you go.

As a person climbs higher, they can survey the surrounding terrain with greater range and clarity. When you apply these metaphors to your own thinking, you can see life from multiple perspectives at once. Then you can choose when to lean in to observe fine details and when to step back to gain a broader perspective. You can choose the thoughts that you want to identify with and those that you wish to detach from. You can put the pieces together to see the trees *and* the forest *and* the remarkable connections between them.

Exercise for Reflection and Journaling

Close your eyes and imagine a part of yourself that is extremely wise, kind, and balanced. This part of yourself sees everything with great objectivity, fairness, understanding, and compassion. Think carefully about this inner presence and consider the following questions:

- How do you visualize the detached observer within yourself? What does this presence look like? How do you picture the place in yourself that can observe everything, hold everything steady, and respond with great understanding, clarity, and compassion?
- How do you feel when you consciously connect with this part of yourself?
- How do you appreciate the value of such a presence within you? How can you express gratitude for this part of yourself? Why is it helpful—and powerful—to draw on the wisdom of this perspective? What does this allow you to see that you couldn't see otherwise?

As always, record your thoughts, feelings, and insights in your journal. As you practice connecting with your impartial spectator, this part of you will become even stronger.

Notes

1 In contrast to the approach featured in this book, the field of Art Therapy approaches the arts as a modality of expression, communication, and healing within a therapeutic context. The bibliography on creative arts therapies is extensive. For discussions of the philosophical, aesthetic, and psychological theories associated with expressive arts therapies, see Paolo J. Knill, Ellen G. Levine, and Stephen K. Levine,

Principles and Practice of Expressive Arts Therapy: Toward a Therapeutic Aesthetics (London: Jessica Kingsley Publishers, 2005). For essays addressing the potential of expressive arts therapies to promote social change, particularly in the wake of collective trauma such as war and political conflict, see Ellen G. Levine and Stephen K. Levine, eds., *Art in Action: Expressive Arts Therapy and Social Change* (London: Jessica Kingsley Publishers, 2011). Regarding the application of neuroscience within the translational practices of art therapy, particularly regarding themes of neuroplasticity, resilience, and trauma, see Juliet L. King and Christianne E. Strang, eds., *Art Therapy and the Neuroscience of Trauma,* 2nd ed. (New York: Routledge, 2024). For an introduction to the various methodological approaches employed in creative arts therapies, see Susan Hogan, *Art Therapy Theories: A Critical Introduction* (London: Routledge, 2016). For a valuable introductory text and reference guide to the theory and practice of art therapy, see Caroline Case et al., *The Handbook of Art Therapy,* 4th ed. (New York: Routledge, 2023). Regarding the use of art therapy methods for the treatment of chronic pain and Post-Traumatic Stress Disorder (PTSD), see Johanne Hamel, *Somatic Art Therapy: Alleviating Pain and Trauma Through Art* (New York: Routledge, 2021). For a sourcebook that approaches art therapy as a means of self-expression and self-understanding by "drawing from within", see Cathy Malchiodi, *Art Therapy Sourcebook*, 2nd ed. (New York: McGraw Hill, 2006). For a discussion of different creative arts practices—including music, dance, visual arts, writing, drama, humor, animal-assisted therapies, and environmental experiences—see Samuel T. Gladding, *The Creative Arts in Counselling*, 5th ed. (Alexandria, VA: American Counselling Association, 2016). Regarding the use of creative arts therapies within LGBTQ communities, see Briana MacWilliam et al., *Creative Arts Therapies and the LGBTQ Community: Theory and Practice* (London: Jessica Kingsley Publishers, 2019).

2 My creative clinical work is situated at the intersection of literary aesthetics and psychosocial oncology. Regarding these subjects, see my books *A Rose from Two Gardens: Saint Thérèse of Lisieux and Images of the End of Life* (San Francisco and Berkeley: University of California Medical Humanities Press, 2022); and *Life at the End of Life: Finding Words Beyond Words* (Bristol, U.K.: Intellect, 2017). My clinical work is sponsored by COLLAGE: Art for Cancer, a nonprofit organization conceived and founded by Dr. Jennifer Wheler. For information on this nonprofit organization, see https://collageforcancer.org.

3 Tudor Balinisteanu, "Summative Comments: What Is Neuroaesthetics?" in *Neuroaesthetics: A Methods-Based Introduction*, eds. Tudor Balinisteanu and Kerry Priest (London: Palgrave Macmillan, 2024), 283.

4 See Robert L. Heilbroner's entry on "Adam Smith", in *The Encyclopaedia Britannica*: https://www.britannica.com/biography/Adam-Smith. The psychiatrist Jeffrey M. Schwartz discusses the importance of the impartial spectator in relation to OCD in *Brain Lock: Free Yourself from Obsessive-Compulsive Behavior* (New York: Harper Perennial, 2016).

References

Balinisteanu, Tudor, and Kerry Priest, eds. *Neuroaesthetics: A Methods-Based Introduction*. London: Palgrave Macmillan. 2024.

Brennan, Marcia. *A Rose From Two Gardens: Saint Thérèse of Lisieux and Images of the End of Life*. San Francisco and Berkeley: University of California Medical Humanities Press. 2022.

Brennan, Marcia. *Life at the End of Life: Finding Words Beyond Words*. Bristol, U.K.: Intellect. 2017.

Case, Caroline, Tessa Dalley, and Dean Reddick. *The Handbook of Art Therapy*. 4th ed. New York: Routledge. 2023.

Gladding, Samuel T. *The Creative Arts in Counselling*. 5th ed. Alexandria, VA: American Counselling Association. 2016.

Hamel, Johanne. *Somatic Art Therapy: Alleviating Pain and Trauma Through Art*. New York: Routledge. 2021.

Heilbroner, Robert L. "Adam Smith." *Encyclopaedia Britannica*. https://www.britannica.com/biography/Adam-Smith

Hogan, Susan. *Art Therapy Theories: A Critical Introduction*. London: Routledge. 2016.

King, Juliet L., and Christianne E. Strang, eds. *Art Therapy and the Neuroscience of Trauma*. 2nd ed. New York: Routledge. 2024.

Knill, Paolo J., Ellen G. Levine, and Stephen K. Levine. *Principles and Practice of Expressive Arts Therapy: Toward a Therapeutic Aesthetics*. London: Jessica Kingsley Publishers. 2005.

Levine, Ellen G., and Stephen K. Levine, eds. *Art in Action: Expressive Arts Therapy and Social Change.* London: Jessica Kingsley Publishers. 2011.

MacWilliam, Briana, Brian T. Harris, Dana George Trottier, and Kristin Long. *Creative Arts Therapies and the LGBTQ Community: Theory and Practice.* London: Jessica Kingsley Publishers. 2019.

Malchiodi, Cathy. *Art Therapy Sourcebook.* 2nd ed. New York: McGraw Hill. 2006.

Schwartz, Jeffrey M. *Brain Lock: Free Yourself From Obsessive-Compulsive Behavior.* New York: Harper Perennial. 2016.

Chapter 4: Knocking Down Dams and Reuniting Rivers

Moving Stuck Energies

Freedom has its own kind of flow, its own kind of rhythm, and its own kind of power.

Figure 4.1

DOI: 10.4324/9781003626725-5

It Shimmers Very Nicely

Freedom is energy in motion. It feels fluid and expansive. Think about how powerful it is to have some space to move around in. You can feel the energy in your own mind and in your own body. When you break a bone, a doctor will often put you in a plaster cast to protect the injured area while it heals. When you finally get the heavy cast off, then you can move again. When you first move, it's like, "Oooh, ow, that hasn't moved for so long!" And then there's the sense of release and the sigh of relief, and everything feels so much better. There's flow once again.

Sometimes we can get stuck in our patterns of thinking. This book can show you how to go into these stuck places and get the energy moving again. You can picture these processes metaphorically. Sometimes in nature, bodies of water become blocked as dams are built to hold back the flow of a river. If the dams are dismantled, then the water can flow freely again. Reading this book can feel a bit like knocking down dams and reuniting rivers in your own mind. As you clear the stuck places, it may feel a bit like: "Ooooh! Ow! Ahhhhh . . . Wonderful! Now, there's movement. There's flow once again . . .".

Sometimes in life, people find themselves living in highly constrained situations that impact both their mind and their body. Within my clinical work, I often meet people who are living in such challenging circumstances. For many years I have worked with people who are battling aggressive cancer or who are facing the very end of their life from this disease. In these difficult situations, people will often tell me stories about what they value most in life, and what is closest to their heart. Sometimes I will simply ask the person, "What is the most beautiful thing you've ever seen, in your entire life?" As the person speaks, I write down their words exactly as they state them, and I put their phrases into successive lines that resemble nonrhyming poetry. I then give the words back to the person as a gift for themselves and their family.

Sometimes people tell powerful stories about freedom and expansion. One day I met a very brave, middle-aged man who had just received a stem cell transplant for a rare and aggressive form of blood cancer. Like all transplantation oncology patients, this man had to stay in his hospital room for several weeks following the procedure. Because he loved being outdoors, the sense of confinement was extremely hard for him. When I asked the man about his special imagery, he told me a story about the forest and the water. Here are his words:

Unfettered Freedom: It Shimmers Very Nicely

Having been in this hospital for several weeks,
The idea of unfettered freedom is precious to me.

My image is of a canoe.
I'm an outdoorsy kind of guy.
A very good friend has a rowboat and a canoe.
He and I go out on the water together.
To get there, you walk down a hill and cross a ridge,

Which is under a canopy of maples and evergreens.
Then you descend to a small grove,
And the green canoe is upside down.
The person steering the canoe gets in first,
And the one doing the power pulling gets in next.
You glide through the underbrush, into the water.
The water is dark green and brown,
And when the sun shines in the summer,
It shimmers very nicely.

This is the pure joy of being out in nature,
And being out on the water.
For me, the forest is as much of a church as the
church is.
I see the beauty in all that has been created.
It's unfettered freedom.
It shimmers very nicely.

When I read the man's words aloud, he said that he felt a sense of peace and a oneness with the world while spending time in nature. While his experience was very powerful, today many people have only limited access to, or interest in, such nature-based experiences. Yet studies have shown both the therapeutic and the developmental benefits associated with engaging with the natural world. Neuroscientists have also identified a link between a person's response to beauty in general, and to the natural environment, in particular.[1] When we become anxious or stuck, it can be very powerful to remember the man's insight that unfettered freedom feels like being out on the water, and that it shimmers very nicely.

The Fluidity of the Watercolor Medium

In the illustration accompanying this chapter, a bright yellow bulldozer is shown dismantling a concrete dam that has been blocking the flow of a river. Because the dam is already partially demolished, the water can begin to flow more freely. This scene is set in a lush green forest, where a stately mansion appears perched on a distant ridge. We'll be examining the mansion in detail in the next chapter. Because watercolor is a fluid medium, it inherently evokes a sense of flow. In this image, the underlying calligraphic linework creates the contours of a natural landscape, including the outlines of the dam, the bulldozer, and the mansion. Paradoxically, the underlying ink lines are both very precise and very fluid. The surrounding trees are created through soft layers of watercolor washes of light yellow-green and dark pine green. The crumbling dam and the flowing water are presented through modulated layers of dull grayish-brown and vibrant turquoise blue. Much as in the opening landscape, an entire world comes into being through the interplay of such intricate lines and soft washes. Together they form the individual details *and* the larger patterns of an image that has its own kind of flow, its own kind of freedom, and its own kind of power.

Stylistically, watercolors are often loose and abstracted. That is, they tend not to feature the type of meticulous illusionism found within highly polished oil paintings. Instead, watercolors frequently display flexible structures with porous boundaries. As such, these abstracted artworks can provide compelling metaphors for envisioning fluid states of mind. Anxiety and OCD are often associated with a rigid approach to life and a tendency toward perfectionism. Whether or not you are living with these conditions, the fluid structures of watercolors offer a new way to envision the themes of flexibility, flow, ease, grace, and transformation.[2]

The Same Emotions Arise, Both in Art and in Life

We've covered a lot of ground in this chapter, but there's still one more subject to consider. In the bestselling book *Your Brain on Art*, Susan Magsamen and Ivy Ross note that "[A]dvances in technology allow us to study human physiology like never before", including how "the aesthetic experiences that make up every moment alter our basic biology". Scientific studies also show how the arts "can help address serious physical and mental health issues, with remarkable results. And they can both help you learn and flourish".[3]

We now know that the emotions a person experiences when encountering works of art are the same ones that they experience in everyday life. In *Feeling Beauty: The Neuroscience of Aesthetic Experience,* the scholar and scientist G. Gabrielle Starr has commented on how aesthetic experiences relate to various systems of the brain. As she observes:

Inquiry into the neuroscience of aesthetics can give us insight into, and lead to new questions about, emotion, the adaptability of neural structures in different individuals, and the relations between complex neural systems ranging from those underpinning imagery to those supporting memory and identity.[4]

Just as works of visual and literary art engage areas of the brain relating to thinking and feeling, emotion and reward, these same creative works can help to change our perceptions of life, and to integrate our inner and outer worlds.

While different readers will respond in different ways to the imaginative artworks featured throughout this book, the flexible structures of the poems and paintings offer innovative perspectives on the themes of fluidity, creativity, and transformation. Just think about how powerful it is to knock down a dam and reunite a river. For some, this may feel like freedom, and it may shimmer *very nicely*. . . .

Exercise for Reflection and Journaling

In the next chapters, we will be examining what neuroscience teaches us about the brain's response to poetry. Before reading that chapter, you may want to experiment with the ways in which poetry can help you to know your own mind. Go back and re-read the poems featured in the first chapters of this book. Choose the one that speaks to you most directly. When you come to the last line, consider:

- If I were to continue writing the poem, what words would come next? Where do I see the poem going?

Where is the land, and where is the water? Where am I standing, and where is the light falling? Where are the shadows, and where are the clearings? How does the landscape transform in my mind's eye? Where do the pathways lead, and why do they lead there?

Follow the words off the page. Consciously track your own responses the way a tracker would follow a trail in the forest.

While such creations are powerful, absolutely *everyone* can do this. Whether you choose to work with poetry, painting, music, design, or any other medium, everyone has the capacity to engage art as a means of self-knowledge and self-creation.

Notes

1 See Pärttyli Rinne et al., "Six Types of Love Differentially Recruit Reward and Social Cognition Brain Areas", *Cerebral Cortex* 34, no. 8 (August 2024): https://pubmed.ncbi.nlm.nih.gov/39183646/. Some of the brain regions that become activated when subjects contemplate nature are also those associated with the viewing of visual imagery. They include the fusiform and parahippocampal gyri, the superior and inferior parietal lobes, and the cuneus. Regarding the ways in which aesthetic experience is distinct from other types of lived experience, see Anjan Chatterjee and Eileen R. Cardillo, "Epilogue: Where Are We Now, and Where Are We Going?" in *Brain, Beauty, & Art:*

Essays Bringing Neuroaesthetics into Focus, ed. Anjan Chatterjee and Eileen R. Cardillo (New York: Oxford University Press, 2022), 235–240.

2 From a different perspective, the literary genre of Graphic Medicine draws on texts and images to convey the experiences of both patients and caregivers. Graphic Medicine engages "the use of comics to tell personal stories of illness and health", and to share experiences in the healthcare system and strategies of coping. See the website produced by the National Library of Medicine: https://www.nlm.nih.gov/exhibition/graphicmedicine/index.html

Within the genre, Jason Adam Katzenstein's book *Everything Is an Emergency: An OCD Story in Words and Pictures* (New York: Harper Perennial, 2020) deftly uses comics to address issues concerning anxiety, OCD, mental health, and the journey toward healing. Another classic text is Ian Williams's *Bad Doctor: The Troubled Life and Times of Dr. Iwan James* (College Park, PA: Penn State University Press, 2015). Williams is himself a medical doctor, a graphic artist, and the founder of the Graphic Medicine website.

3 Susan Magsamen and Ivy Ross, *Your Brain on Art: How the Arts Transform Us* (New York: Random House, 2023), x.

4 G. Gabrielle Starr, *Feeling Beauty: The Neuroscience of Aesthetic Experience* (Cambridge, MA: MIT Press, 2015), xii, 41. For an explanation of the neurological processes involved in aesthetic experience, see pp. 24–25 of this volume.

References

Chatterjee, Anjan, and Eileen R. Cardillo, eds. *Brain, Beauty, & Art: Essays Bringing Neuroaesthetics into Focus.* New York: Oxford University Press. 2022.

Katzenstein, Jason Adam. *Everything is an Emergency: An OCD Story in Words and Pictures.* New York: Harper Perennial. 2020.

Magsamen, Susan, and Ivy Ross. *Your Brain on Art: How the Arts Transform Us.* New York: Random House. 2023.

Rinne, Pärttyli, Juha M. Lahnakoski, Heini Saarimäki, Mikke Tavast, Mikko Sams, and Linda Henriksson. "Six Types of Love Differentially Recruit Reward and Social Cognition Brain Areas." *Cerebral Cortex* 34, no. 8 (August 2024). https://pubmed.ncbi.nlm.nih.gov/39183646/

Starr, G. Gabrielle. *Feeling Beauty: The Neuroscience of Aesthetic Experience.* Cambridge, MA: MIT Press. 2015.

Williams, Ian. *Bad Doctor: The Troubled Life and Times of Dr. Iwan James.* College Park, PA: Penn State University Press. 2015.

Chapter 5: Your Brain Is a Mansion

Neurotransmission Within Majestic Wired Architecture

Much like a stately mansion, your brain is a majestic form of wired architecture.

Figure 5.1

DOI: 10.4324/9781003626725-6

The Mansion of the Brain

A mansion is a "dwelling place". This can be a permanent home, or it can be a "relay on a major route", such as a resting point along a journey.[1] A mansion can be a physical space, or it can be a subtle state of consciousness. You can always dwell in the mansion of your own thoughts.

The watercolor appearing at the beginning of this chapter depicts a regal stone mansion all lit up at night. Stars sparkle under an indigo sky, while soft golden light radiates in the mansion's many windows. If you look closely, you'll see that the building's stone façade is surrounded by a transparent silhouette of the human brain. The brainstem sinks into the ground, while the crown—the highest point in the skull—merges with the stars above.

On various levels, this is an image of illumination. Inside the mansion, each room contains a light switch. When the switch is turned on, the light gives off a warm golden glow. When the mind lights up, it is like turning on little lights in little rooms inside the mansion of the brain.

Some books and paintings are so powerful,
They can feel alive.
When you read such a book, you can feel the power of
the words
Coming alive in your own mind,
Illuminating your thinking and igniting new ideas inside
of you.

When you read such a book,
You can almost feel a surge of energy.
As the ideas are transmitted,
And the words and images move through you,
They transform into something that your mind
can grasp.
Then you can see the story from your own perspective.
You can begin to relate the words and images to your
own experiences,
To your own wisdom,
To your own understanding,
To what you have been exposed to,
And to what you have integrated within your own
experience.
As this happens, it is like little switches being turned on
in the mind.

When the light is flicked on,
You might think, "Oh, I remember, I once had an
experience
That reminds me of what I'm reading right now . . ."
The words and images all light up different parts
of your brain,
To bring emotions,
To bring memory,
And to bring understanding.
The connections are ignited,
Like little lights in little rooms
Inside the mansion of your brain.

Connections Light Connections: Neurotransmission and Action Potentials

Neurons contain dendrites, which are the short branching fibers that conduct impulses *toward* a cell body. Neurons also contain axons, which are the long, threadlike filaments that conduct impulses *away* from a cell body, toward other cells. Dendrites are associated with incoming energy, and axons are associated with outgoing impulses. The two structures work together to receive and transmit energy. When energy moves through the circuits of neurons, the connections can be envisioned as networks of light.

This illustration depicts energies being exchanged between two neurons, as the axons of one neuron connect with the dendrites of another.[2] The areas of connection are called synapses. The prefix, *syn*, means "with or together", while the root, *apse*, indicates a point of joining. Within the brain, a synapse is the junction between two nerve cells. A synapse consists of three elements: a presynaptic ending, which contains neurotransmitters and other biological materials; a postsynaptic ending, which contains receptor sites, or places where neurotransmitters can be received; and a synaptic cleft, which is a tiny bit of space between the nerve cell endings. Neurons release chemical messengers, or neurotransmitters, into the synapses, which allows the neurons to communicate with one another.

The process of connection is called neurotransmission, and it involves both chemistry and electricity. Just as neurotransmitters contain highly specialized chemicals,

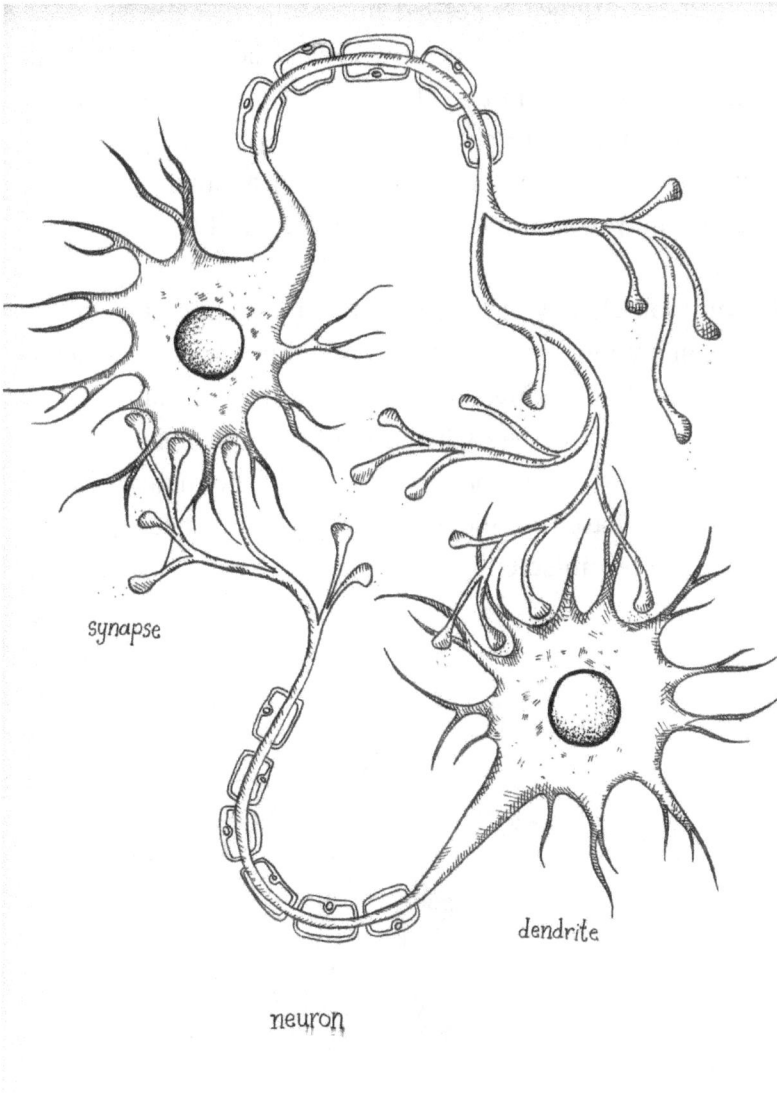

synapse

dendrite

neuron

Figure 5.2

an electrical trigger is needed for communication between cells. An electrical impulse must travel down an axon to its presynaptic ending. This triggers a reaction, and neurotransmitters are released into the synaptic cleft. There they can bind with the receptor sites of another nerve cell, such as the postsynaptic ending of a dendrite.[3]

If you look closely at the pattern of light appearing in the mansion's windows, you'll see something special—namely, you'll see the peaking form of an action potential. An action potential occurs when an electrical signal travels through an axon. The pattern of light in the mansion's windows is based on the actual structures of neuronal firing, as seen in scientific imaging studies.[4]

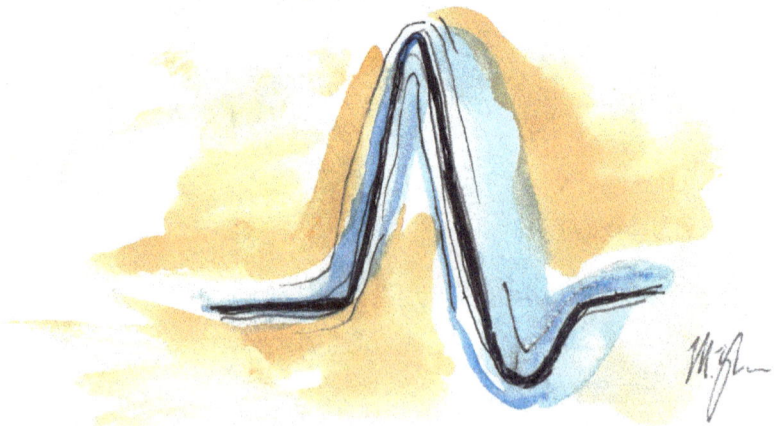

Figure 5.3

The pattern of energy transfer in an action potential resembles a peaking form with a crest and a trough, which represent the high and the low points of the wave, respectively.[5] In this drawing the action potential appears as a spiky calligraphic black line surrounded by vibrant shades of blue and gold. Just as the drawing is scientifically accurate, it evokes the kind of imaginative energy associated with epiphanies and illuminations. The drawing thus provides a complementary way to visualize little lights being turned on in little rooms inside the mansion of the brain.

The Poetry of the Networked Brain

When describing the architecture of the networked brain, G. Gabrielle Starr has noted that

[a]esthetic experience relies on a distributed neural architecture, a set of brain areas involved in emotion, perception, imagery, memory, and language. But more than this, aesthetic experience emerges from *networked* interactions, the workings of intricately connected and coordinated brain systems that, together, form a flexible architecture enabling us to develop new arts and to see the world around us differently. Systems for emotion and reward, along with the default mode network (an interconnected set of brain areas that contributes to our sense of self-identity, as well as to our ability to imagine other worlds and other people, among other

functions), work to enact the necessarily dynamic, constantly reevaluative neural processes that underpin aesthetic life.[6]

We now live in an age of unprecedented technological development. Innovations such as functional magnetic resonance imaging (fMRI) technologies enable us to see what is happening inside the brain as people respond to different types of stimuli, including to works of art. Semir Zeki, one of the pioneering figures in the field of neuroaesthetics, found that a particular area of the brain—the medial orbitofrontal cortex—lights up when a person perceives beauty. As Zeki observed, "We know that aesthetic experience correlates with activity in the medial orbitofrontal cortex regardless of its source", whether the beauty is perceived in visual art, music, or mathematics.[7] In the silhouette of the brain appearing at the beginning of this chapter, the medial orbitofrontal cortex is located along the left-hand side of the building, below the slanting black roof of the furthest tower (see also *Figure 9.1*).

Scientific studies have also shown that literature lights up the brain. As one researcher has observed, "the complexities with which our brain constructs the world in and around us [occur] because [literature] unifies thought and language, music and imagery in a clear, manageable way, most often with play, pleasure, and emotion".[8] As you read these words and look at the paintings, new insights and connections may be ignited inside of you. This may be like turning on little lights in little rooms inside the mansion of the brain.

Exercise for Reflection and Journaling

In your journal, consider the following questions:

- How do you envision the mansion of your brain? How would you begin to picture this majestic form of wired architecture? What style would the building be? How does the mansion's exterior surface relate to its inner structures and patterns? Can you imagine drawing a floorplan of the mansion of your brain? Can you imagine drawing an elevation, or vertical view, of the building's façade? What makes the mansion uniquely your own? What makes it uniquely beautiful?
- Why is it powerful to see your brain as a functional living environment *and* as a complex, living work of art?
- How do you dwell in the mansion of your own thoughts? How would you describe your own style of thinking?
- If you were to write a poem about these subjects, how would you begin?

Inside the mansion of my brain,
I see and feel. . . .

Notes

1 See the etymology and definitions of the word "mansion" in the *OED*: https://www.oed.com/dictionary/mansion_n?tab=etymology&tl=true#37961414 and https://www.oed.com/dictionary/mansion_n?tab=meaning_and_use&tl=true#37961414

2 This diagram depicts an axodendritic synapse, as the axons of one neuron connect with the dendrites of another. In addition, neurons can form axosomatic synapses when an axon connects with the body of another cell, and they can form axoaxonic synapses when the axons of two neurons connect with each other.

3 Regarding these processes, see Kendra Cherry's articles on "Neurons and Their Role in the Nervous System" and "Action Potential and How Neurons Fire": https://www.verywellmind.com/what-is-a-neuron-2794890 and https://www.verywellmind.com/what-is-an-action-potential-2794811

4 Regarding the morphological reference points of segmented neurons, see Boglarka H. Varkuti et al., "Neuron-based High-content Assay and Screen for CNS Active Mitotherapeutics", *Science Advances* 6, no. 2 (January 2020): eaaw8702.

5 An "action potential" is a physiological term that signifies "a wave of electrical activity which is propagated through a nerve fibre or other excitable cell by the successive temporary depolarization of adjacent regions of the membrane". See the entry on "action potential" in the *OED*: https://www.oed.com/dictionary/action-potential_n?tab=meaning_and_use#9919916017

6 G. Gabrielle Starr, *Feeling Beauty: The Neuroscience of Aesthetic Experience* (Cambridge, MA: MIT Press, 2015), xv.

7 Semir Zeki is quoted in Faith A. Pak and Ethan B. Reichsman, "Beauty and the Brain: The Emerging Field of Neuroaesthetics", *The Harvard Crimson* (November 10, 2017): https://www.thecrimson.com/

article/2017/11/10/neuroaesthetics-cover/. Neuroaesthetic studies have also shown that the brain's visual cortex responds to beauty in a consistent fashion when a person is presented with various types of subjects, from utilitarian objects to the faces of people appearing in portraits. Regarding these subjects, see Marius A. Teodorescu, "Neuroaesthetic Approaches to the Visual Arts—Creation," in *Neuroaesthetics: A Methods-Based Introduction*, eds. Tudor Balinisteanu and Kerry Priest (London: Palgrave Macmillan, 2024), 116–118. Regarding the specific brain regions associated with various responses to the perception of visual beauty, scientists have observed significant activity in the left dorsolateral prefrontal cortex (DLPC), and they have further noted that the ventromedial prefrontal cortex (vmPFC) can become activated when subjects respond to particular types of visual beauty, including images of faces and natural landscapes. Regarding these studies, see Eric Munar and Camilo J. Cela-Conde, "The Role of Left Dorsolateral Prefrontal Cortices in Aesthetic Valuation", and Teresa Pegors, "Kinds of Beauty and the Prefrontal Cortex", in *Brain, Beauty, & Art: Essays Bringing Neuroaesthetics into Focus*, eds. Anjan Chatterjee and Eileen R. Cardillo (New York: Oxford University Press, 2022), chapters 19 and 14.

8 Neuroaesthetic studies have led researchers to conclude that "the pleasure that people experience from looking at beautiful objects (including sentences) automatically recruits parts of the brain's general reward circuitry", particularly in the amygdala and the nucleus accumbens. See Arthur M. Jacobs, "Neurocognitive

poetics: Methods and Models for Investigating the Neuronal and Cognitive-Affective Bases of Literature Reception", *Frontiers in Human Neuroscience* 9 (April 2015): https://www.frontiersin.org/articles/10.3389/fnhum.2015.00186/full

References

Chatterjee, Anjan, and Eileen R. Cardillo, eds. *Brain, Beauty, & Art: Essays Bringing Neuroaesthetics into Focus.* New York: Oxford University Press. 2022.

Cherry, Kendra. "Action Potential and How Neurons Fire." *Verywellmind.* https://www.verywellmind.com/what-is-an-action-potential-2794811

Cherry, Kendra. "Neurons and Their Role in the Nervous System." *Verywellmind.* https://www.verywellmind.com/what-is-a-neuron-2794890

Jacobs, Arthur M. "Neurocognitive Poetics: Methods and Models for Investigating the Neuronal and Cognitive-affective Bases of Literature Reception." *Frontiers in Human Neuroscience* 9 (April 2015). https://www.frontiersin.org/articles/10.3389/fnhum.2015.00186/full

Pak, Faith A., and Ethan B. Reichsman. "Beauty and the Brain: The Emerging Field of Neuroaesthetics." *The Harvard Crimson,* November 10, 2017. https://www.thecrimson.com/article/2017/11/10/neuroaesthetics-cover/

Simpson, J.A., and E.S.C. Weiner, eds. *The Oxford English Dictionary.* 2nd ed. Oxford: Clarendon Press. 1989.

Starr, G. Gabrielle. *Feeling Beauty: The Neuroscience of Aesthetic Experience.* Cambridge, MA: MIT Press. 2015.

Teodorescu, Marius A. "Neuroaesthetic Approaches to the Visual Arts—Creation." In *Neuroaesthetics: A Methods-Based Introduction*, edited by Tudor Balinisteanu and Kerry Priest, 116–118. London: Palgrave Macmillan, 2024.

Varkuti, Boglarka H., Miklos Kepiro, Ze Liu, Kyle Vick, Yosef Avchalumov, Rodrigo Pacifico, Courtney M. MacMullen, Theodore M. Kamenecka, Sathyanarayanan V. Puthanveettil, and Ronald L. Davis. "Neuron-based High-content Assay and Screen for CNS Active Mitotherapeutics." *Science Advances* 6, no. 2 (January 2020): eaaw8702.

Chapter 6: A Wetland in the Forest

Neurotransmitters and Synaptic Junctions

Let's begin with an image of a beautiful wetland in a forest. . . .

Figure 6.1

DOI: 10.4324/9781003626725-7

The Magic of Microenvironments

In the brain, specialized fluids called neurotransmitters flow through the pathways between the neurons or nerve cells. Neurotransmitters are streams of chemicals that carry messages across these fluid-filled spaces, which are called synaptic junctions. You can think of the junctions between neurons as microenvironments, or miniature worlds. Viewed metaphorically, the relationship between the brain and its neurotransmitters is a bit like the relationship between a forest and its ponds and streams and all the plants and animals that move through and flow across these pathways.

Neurotransmitters flow in a way that is very different from the flow of blood. The blood that flows through our bodies is more like a river, moving from one place to another at a particular rate, depth, and speed. Neurotransmitters are more like a beautiful wetland in a forest. All sorts of chemical reactions move information across a wetland. These reactions are brought about by many layers of organisms, from the tiniest to the biggest.

Imagine a wetland stream that contains
Plant cellular organisms and animal cellular organisms,
From the tiniest, single-celled organisms
To complex, multi-celled creatures.

The pond holds so much life.
A fish swims through the pond.
Then an otter swims through.
Then a moose walks through.

Then some geese fly through.
All of these creatures are transmitting energies
From one place to another.

The energy in a neurotransmitter is similar.
You can think of this as being almost like a pond,
A place where many energies move across and through
The vehicle of the water.
In a wetland, this looks like a process of moving energy
From one organism to another,
Across the wetland,
From one side of the forest to the other.

Balance is key to the system.
When something is in balance,
You can feel it.
And when something is out of balance,
You can feel that, too.

When something is in balance,
You don't give it much attention.
But when a system goes out of balance,
Then you have to pay more attention,
To balance the system as much as you can.

In nature, different energies might be called in to rebalance
a system—
Different rainwater, different winds, different storms,
Different plants, different animals—even humans—
Might be called in to rebalance a system.

The layers of complexity are amazing.
Everything in the system works together.

When everything is in balance,
There is a harmonizing effect that is felt by all.
And when things are out of balance,
There is a disharmony that is also felt by all.

This is all part of a grand composition.
It's mysterious.
It's magical.
It's chemical.
It's scientific.
It's a work of art.
And, it's community.
It's everything.

Communication Pathways and Neural Responses

Within the body, neurotransmitters move chemical streams across nerve endings as they carry messages from a nerve cell to another nerve cell, to a muscle cell, or to a gland.[1] As the cells communicate with one another, neurotransmitters are released into synapses. This process occurs at the end point of an axon, which is called an axon terminal. As we have seen, axons carry energetic impulses away from the cell body, toward other cells. An axon terminal is the end point where the electrical signals of an axon can be converted to chemical signals. This process allows connections to be made between different types of cells.

Within neurons, neurotransmitters are stored in tiny, thin-walled sacs or pouches, which are called synaptic vesicles. The electrical signal from the axon causes the tiny sacs holding the neurotransmitters to fuse with the cell membrane. Neurotransmitters are then released into the synaptic junction—or the tiny, fluid-filled space between individual nerve cells. Chemical messages flow across this space, where they can bind with the receptor of another nearby cell, which is called a target cell.

Once a neuron binds with a target cell, a reaction is triggered. Some reactions cause a neuron to fire; this is called an excitatory response. Some reactions prevent a neuron from firing; this is called an inhibitory response. And some reactions effect how cells communicate with one another; this is called a modulatory response.[2]

Neurotransmitters affect your nervous system and your brain activity. They influence your thinking and your emotions, your memory and your learning, your sleep and your appetite, as well as your perceptions of pain and anxiety, of pleasure and joy. As you can see, the microcosmic spaces within and between neurons shape, and are shaped by, the macrocosm of life. The microcosm and the macrocosm constantly work together to create your world.

In the wetland scene appearing at the beginning of this chapter, an otter swims playfully in a pond, watching a pair of geese fly overhead. Fish swim through the lush blue and green water. The pond is filled with plankton, which are the tiny drifting microorganisms that make their home in the water. The blue and white sky is reflected on the shimmering surface of a pond whose borders are surrounded by soft green trees and lush green grasses. Just as all plants and animals are transmitting energy from one point to another, the spiky silhouettes of the bordering grasses resemble the peaking forms of action potentials.[3] As we saw in Chapter 5, an action potential occurs when an electrical signal travels down an axon and information is transmitted between neurons. Much like the cresting patterns of light appearing in the mansion's windows, the wetland grasses in this landscape display the same peaking patterns of amplitudes and dips found within synaptic transmissions.

The Poetry of Communication

Notably, these same peaking energy patterns are also seen in neuroaesthetic studies on poetry. In one experiment, researchers measured the brain responses of people who read poetry that either was consistent with, or that violated, established poetic rules. While the participants had no prior knowledge of the poetry itself, when they read the sentences that corresponded with the correct formats, they registered the most pronounced "event-related brain potential"—or, the highest degree of energy and "burst of electrical activity"—in the peaking amplitudes of their EEG (electroencephalogram) graphs.[4] The results led the researchers to conclude that humans have a built-in, intuitive sense of poetry.[5] As one of the scientists put it: "Our results argue for a profoundly intuitive origin of poetry. . . . Poetry appears to be 'built in,' it is like a profound intuition, [and] every human being is an unconscious poet".[6]

Whether you are looking at the EEG graphs of people reading poetry, or at the spiky green grasses of the lush wetland scene, or at the arcing pattern of golden light appearing in the mansion's stately windows, you are looking at intricate networks of transmission and communication. This is all part of a grand composition. It is mysterious, magical, chemical, scientific, and a work of art. It's everything.

Exercise for Reflection and Journaling

You can practice visualizing the connections between various points within energetic transmissions. Recall a time when you sent someone a message and received a response. This could be a time when you called someone, or sent an email, or a text, or you mailed someone a birthday card. If you were to imagine this exchange schematically, how would you visualize the networks involved in sending and receiving the messages? Choose one particularly vivid example and consider the following questions:

• When the communication occurred, where were you physically, and where was the other person? Once the image appears clearly in your mind's eye, you can think about the space connecting the two points. While this space might *appear* to be empty, it is filled with dynamic energy. This seemingly empty space represents a corridor of connection and communication.

- How would you describe this interconnected space with another person? If you were to picture this space visually, what does it look like? If you were to graph the patterns of the exchange, where would the peaks and valleys of the energy fall? Would the lines on the graph be dramatically sharp and spiky, or would they be soft and curvy? How do the individual details form larger patterns within the overall pattern of connection and exchange?
- Why is it powerful to visualize the seemingly empty spaces where energetic transmissions occur? Why is it important to be consciously aware of the often-invisible processes that unfold in your brain and in your life?

Notes

1 According to the *OED,* a neurotransmitter is "any chemical substance that is released by a presynaptic nerve ending in response to the arrival of a nerve impulse and crosses the synapse to excite (or inhibit) the postsynaptic cell". See the entry on "neurotransmitter" in the *OED*: https://www.oed.com/dictionary/neurotransmitter_n?tab=meaning_and_use#34677314

2 For discussions of these processes, see the entry on "Neurotransmitters" at https://my.clevelandclinic.org/health/articles/22513-neurotransmitters and Kendra Cherry, "What Are Neurotransmitters?" *Verywellmind*: https://www.verywellmind.com/what-is-a-neurotransmitter-2795394

3 The silhouettes of the marshland grasses appearing in this illustration are based on the graphic patterns of

"simulated muscle fiber action potentials detected at the electrode" for both resistive and conductive skin biosensors. See Johannes P. Van Dijk et al., "Evidence of Potential Averaging over the Finite Surface of a Bioelectrical Surface Electrode", *Annals of Biomedical Engineering* 37 (April 1, 2009): https://www.researchgate.net/figure/Simulated-muscle-fiber-action-potentials-at-the-skin-surface-below-the-electrode-gray_fig4_24232608

4   An electroencephalogram produces "a record of the electrical activity of the brain, typically produced by means of electrodes attached to the scalp". See the entry on "electroencephalogram" in the *OED*: https://www.oed.com/search/dictionary/?scope=Entries&q=electroencephalogram

5   Awel Vaughan-Evans et al., "Implicit Detection of Poetic Harmony by the Naïve Brain", *Frontiers in Psychology* 7 (November 2016): https://www.frontiersin.org/articles/10.3389/fpsyg.2016.01859/full

The researchers concluded, "These results show for the first time that before we even consider literal meaning [of words], the musical properties of poetry instinctively speak to the human mind in ways that escape consciousness".

6   The neuroscientist Guillaume Thierry is quoted in Patrick J. Kiger, "The Human Brain Is Hardwired for Poetry," *Howstuffworks*: https://science.howstuffworks.com/life/inside-the-mind/human-brain/how-poetry-affects-human-brain.htm

References

Cherry, Kendra. "What Are Neurotransmitters?" *Verywellmind*. https://www.verywellmind.com/what-is-a-neurotransmitter-2795394

Kiger, Patrick J. "The Human Brain is Hardwired for Poetry." *Howstuffworks*. https://science.howstuffworks.com/life/inside-the-mind/human-brain/how-poetry-affects-human-brain.htm

Simpson, J.A., and E.S.C. Weiner, eds. *The Oxford English Dictionary*. 2nd ed. Oxford: Clarendon Press. 1989.

Van Dijk, Johannes P., M.M. Lowery, B.G. Lapatki, and D.F. Stegeman. "Evidence of Potential Averaging over the Finite Surface of a Bioelectrical Surface Electrode." *Annals of Biomedical Engineering* 37 (April 1, 2009). https://www.researchgate.net/figure/Simulated-muscle-fiber-action-potentials-at-the-skin-surface-below-the-electrode-gray_fig4_24232608

Vaughan-Evans, Awel, Robat Trefor, Llion Jones, Peredur Lynch, Manon W. Jones, and Guillaume Thierry. "Implicit Detection of Poetic Harmony by the Naïve Brain." *Frontiers in Psychology* 7 (November 2016). https://www.frontiersin.org/articles/10.3389/fpsyg.2016.01859/full

Chapter 7: The Brain of the Forest

Dendrites, Axons, and Synaptic Clefts

Much like nerve cells in the brain, the trees of the forest operate through elaborate systems of networks.

Figure 7.1

DOI: 10.4324/9781003626725-8

Great Webs of Life

In a forest, different plants, mycelium, and the tiny rootlets underneath the earth all work together. The symbiotic relationship between the fungi and the plant roots is called mycorrhizae. Similar processes can be seen in the pathways of the brain. As neurons circulate fluids, minerals, vitamins, and electrical impulses throughout the body, they create structures of connection and communication. This is not unlike what lies underneath the earth—beneath the trees— as information passes along the forest floor to create a sense of balance and communication throughout the entire system.

As Above, So Below

Just as the branching limbs of trees are dendritic, the spaces between the tree roots can be seen as axonal. Within the brain, an axon is a single long nerve cell that carries outgoing impulses. Beneath the forest floor, the roots of the individual trees may touch one another, and there is a tiny bit of space where the roots intersect. As electricity moves across that space, information passes through the earth. The electricity moving across the intersecting spaces of the tree roots can be seen as axonal, just as the tree canopy overhead can be seen as dendritic.

Within the forest, one tree may be up against another tree of the same species, or it may be adjacent to a tree of a different species. Energetic exchanges can occur both within and between tree species. In the forest, these

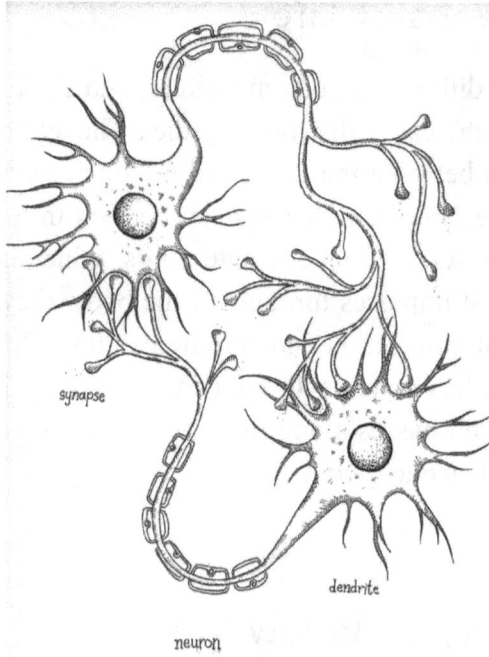

Figure 7.2

Figure 7.3

exchanges occur in the spaces between plant roots. In the brain, these exchanges occur in areas that are called synaptic clefts. Synaptic clefts are the tiny gaps and junctions where individual neurons communicate with one another. Just as the ground of the forest can be seen as an interconnected synaptic field, the communications and connections that thread through the forest floor can be seen metaphorically as the "brain of the forest".

Arborization is the framework of natural life.
It is seen in the interconnectedness of the body,
And in the interconnectedness of the forest.

Branching, treelike structures appear in the veins of the body,
Within the nervous system,
And in the neurons of the brain.
They are also found in the roots beneath a tree,
And in the branches overhead.

In a tree, the roots beneath the crown,
And the branches that reach to the heavens,
Can be a perfect reflection of one another.
Some artists have painted images of trees reflected in the water.
When you see such a painting,
It's as though two worlds are visible at the same time—
The one above the ground, and the one below.

What is seen below the ground is often in perfect balance
With what is seen above the ground:
A branch grows to the right,
A root grows to the right.

If a branch grows into the tree next to it,
The roots may also grow into the tree next to it.
The two realms often mirror one another.

Interconnectedness is the basis of life.
With anything that you look at,
At the base,
There is a web of connection.
This is happening on all levels,
Seen and unseen.
It is the great web of life.

Just as the brain organizes, analyzes, and transfers information, these processes unfold through intricate networks of communication. In a forest, transfers of energy and information are also pervasive, as creatures may warn one another of a dangerous predator, or they may display a remarkable ability to sense natural disasters. Both the brain and the forest are living systems that regularly engage in complex transfers of energy and information.

Just as a forest is always changing, human moods, feelings, and states of mind are constantly shifting, as well. Emotions ebb and flow with the circumstances of life through both stressful events and joyous ones. The inherently dynamic nature of life can be seen within the neuronal signals of the body and in the natural cycles and seasonal changes of a forest. Maintaining this larger perspective can help you to see the value of life's experiences and to keep the bigger picture in mind as you consider both the forest and the trees and the multitude of connections between them.

Envisioning Connections

One day I met an elderly man who was facing the very end of his life. When I asked the man about the images that were close to his heart, he recalled the profound sense of connection that he experienced while visiting the temperate rainforests of the West Coast of the United States. As the man spoke, I wrote down his words exactly as he stated them and assembled the words into a poem:

To Be Engaged with the Forest

I'm thinking of the mountains.
At the lower elevations,
There are temperate rain forests,
With lots of old growth trees, mosses, and ferns.
There are not many old growth forests left.

Being there, it felt like there are spiritual things
That are only there,
That are not in other places.
The trees all exist and communicate with each other.
It was so peaceful,
To be engaged with the forest.

Much like the watercolor painting appearing at the beginning of this chapter, the man's story is filled with images of ancient forests, majestic trees, and distant mountains. Lush greens and soft browns create the tonal keynotes of both landscapes, which are full of abundant leaves, curving tree trunks, and delicate ferns and mosses.

In both the painting and the poem, the natural imagery is physical *and* subtle, grounded *and* visionary. As the man described the sense of spirituality that he experienced in the forest, he recalled an overall sense of oneness with life itself. As he spoke, I listened closely and saw how the man became very peaceful as he reflected on these interconnected layers of being and presence.

Interwoven Fields of Poetry and Prose

If the man's words were presented in a prose format instead of a poetic one, they would appear like this:

> I'm thinking of the mountains. At the lower elevations, there are temperate rain forests, with lots of old growth trees, mosses, and ferns. There are not many old growth forests left. Being there, it felt like there are spiritual things that are only there, that are not in other places. The trees all exist and communicate with each other. It was so peaceful, to be engaged with the forest.

Prose appeals to the human story. When a person reads prose, the words interact with the reader's emotions and experiences, including the ones they have had and the ones they would like to have. Prose can light up a person's frontal cortex and their limbic system (we will examine these structures in detail in the following chapters). When people read prose, the nervous system becomes engaged because the heart opens and people get tensed in their whole body, anxious to hear what comes next. Sometimes readers soften into their memories, as the nervous system creates associations between what is known and what is desired.

When the same words appear in a poetic format, the cadence and imagery can open up a different sense of unity and connection. The flow of poetic language can light a person's heart and ignite their relationship to beauty and to an overall sense of oneness. When we encounter something that is beautiful, we can become more open to *all* that is beautiful, both inside and outside ourselves—much like the networked structures of the brain's synaptic field, or like the roots that thread through a forest floor.

Exercise for Reflection and Journaling

You can experiment with creating complex, interwoven landscapes. You can begin by asking someone what is beautiful and meaningful for them. As the person speaks, write down their words exactly as they state them. When they have finished, transcribe their statement into prose, and then read the words back to them, allowing them to make any corrections or changes that they wish. Then translate the same words into a poetic format, allowing the line breaks to fall naturally, based on the person's patterns of breath, thought, and speech. When you are finished, share the artwork with the person as a way of thanking them. Importantly, the person telling the story is the owner of the narrative. Their story should not be shared unless they expressly give permission to do so. The confidence and wishes of the speaker should *always* be respected.

- Once you have the two creative expressions, consider what they have in common, and how they are different. How is each format uniquely powerful as a mode of transmission, connection, and communication? One of my students once observed that prose makes the words feel more condensed, while poetry makes the same words feel more expansive. As a result, prose invites reflection, while poetry demands presence.
- As you are speaking with the person, messages are continually being transmitted and received across a shared field of exchange. In your mind's eye, you can picture images of dendrites as you receive incoming information and axons as you send outgoing responses.
- Why is it powerful to experiment with such complementary modes of expression? How do they shape your perspective on life? How is this all part of the art of transformation?

Chapter 8: Footsteps and Shoe Mending

Neuronal Pathways and Hebb's Rule

When you walk through the mud, your footsteps leave a trail. So too do your thoughts leave a neuronal trail in your own brain.

Figure 8.1

DOI: 10.4324/9781003626725-9

A Journey Made Up of Thoughts

Within the brain, neurons are nerve cells that both receive and transmit information. The origin of the word "neuron" relates to nerve, sinew, cord, and tendon, and the example given in the *Oxford English Dictionary* refers to cobblers and shoe-menders. Such images are closely associated with paths and pathways. A path is "a way or track formed by the continued treading of pedestrians or animals", especially by "people on foot". A pathway is also "a fixed route formed by a chain of nerve cells and along which impulses of a particular kind usually travel".[1] When you think a thought or practice an action, chains of neurons are activated in your brain. It's like you are undertaking a journey made up of thoughts. As your footsteps fall along a pathway, they leave a neuronal trail.

Hebb's Rule: Neurons That Fire Together, Wire Together

In 1949, the neuropsychologist Donald O. Hebb wrote an influential book entitled *The Organization of Behavior: A Neuropsychological Theory*. As Hebb examined the physiology of the human brain and its learning processes, he found that "behavior and neural function are perfectly correlated". Hebb observed that repeated patterns of thoughts and behaviors reinforce the interconnected pathways between neurons. As he put it: "Any two cells or systems of cells that are repeatedly active at the same time will tend to become 'associated,' so that activity in one facilitates activity in the other".[2] As a result, when the axon of one cell repeatedly fires the axon of a nearby cell, the efficiency of the cell firing increases, and the connection between the two cells is strengthened. As the cells are repeatedly activated, they grow together, and their associated pathways become reinforced. Phrased simply, Hebb's rule is known as "neurons that fire together, wire together".

When you practice a skill, such as learning a language, or riding a bicycle, or playing a musical instrument, over time your movements become smoother, more graceful, and more efficient as the related neural pathways become reinforced. Just as repetition entrenches the patterns that you want to cultivate, unfortunately the same is also true for the patterns that you do not want to cultivate. This is why OCD can be such a stubborn condition. The repetition of distressing behaviors—such as constantly checking locks or scrubbing hands—entrenches the pattern. The more that the pattern is repeated, the more entrenched the pathways become, and the harder the pattern is to alter. We will examine these themes in detail in Part Two.

Visualizing the Trails of Thought

The watercolor at the beginning of this chapter presents a suggestive metaphor for envisioning these subjects. When viewed under a microscope, a neuron appears like a cell with trailing end-branches. In this watercolor, the trails formed by a person's thoughts are imaginatively presented as a stylized pair of shoes walking along a branching pathway. The rich brown earth, the lush green forest, and the golden sunlight all evoke a sense of groundedness. In this landscape, a figure stands in the soma, or cell body, of a neuron, looking down at the sinews and tendons of her feet. As she gazes ahead, she can anticipate the pattern that her footsteps will make as she walks along a dendritic pathway. Each step creates a connection that weaves a larger pattern. The more a pathway is taken, the more deeply entrenched the pattern becomes.

This vivid metaphor can help you to envision the pathways created by your thoughts and actions. If there is a pattern that you want to change, you can always think of altering your thoughts and behaviors as a creative form of "shoe-mending". In time, this will allow you to make a different journey.

Exercise for Reflection and Journaling

- Take a moment to observe your familiar patterns of thought and behavior. What do you notice? How does one idea lead to the next in your own mind? You can begin this exploration by considering how you approach a positive behavior, such as how you practice a sport that you love, or how you rehearse for a play that you're excited to be in, or how you go about learning a new language. How do you establish and reinforce the positive patterns of thought and behavior that you wish to cultivate?
- If you were to approach the subject metaphorically, how would you imagine your own inner pathways of

thought, and the related trails of your behaviors, when you engage in these activities? Do they appear like deer trails through the woods? Or do they look like something else? What forms do they take? What colors are they? What makes these patterns uniquely your own? Why is this reflection so powerful?

- To take this exploration further, think for a moment about the creative possibilities that lie within all sorts of natural patterns, such as the currents of the oceans or the winds, the shifting orbits of the stars, the shapes and colors of birds' wings, the topographical maps of cities, or the complex living world contained in a single drop of blood. As you can see, the image of deer trails through the woods provides just one way to picture the physical and metaphorical patterns that thread through life. There are many other possibilities, as well. Which metaphors appeal to you and why?

Notes

1 Regarding the definitions of "neuron", "neuro-", "path", and "pathway", see the entries on these terms in the *OED*: https://www.oed.com/dictionary/neuron_n?tab=e tymology#34672384; https://www.oed.com/dictionary/ neuro_combform?tab=etymology#34665843; https:// www.oed.com/dictionary/path_n1?tab=meaning_and_use; and https://www.oed.com/dictionary/ pathway_n?tab=meaning_and_use#31764924

2 Donald O. Hebb, *The Organization of Behavior: A Neuropsychological Theory* (New York: Wiley, 1949), xiii, 70: https://pure.mpg.de/rest/items/item_2346268_3/

component/file_2346267/content Regarding these concepts, Hebb wrote:

> Let us assume that the persistence or repetition of a reverberatory activity (or 'trace') tends to induce lasting cellular changes that add to its stability. . . . When an axon of cell *A* is near enough to excite a cell *B* and repeatedly or persistently takes part in firing it, some growth process or metabolic change takes place in one or both cells such that *A*'s efficiency, as one of the cells firing *B*, is increased.

For a discussion of the history of this concept preceding Hebb's theory, see Richard E. Brown et al., "The Hebb Synapse Before Hebb: Theories of Synaptic Function in Learning and Memory Before Hebb (1949)", *Frontiers in Behavioral Neuroscience* 15 (October 2021): https://www.frontiersin.org/articles/10.3389/fnbeh.2021.732195/full

References

Brown, Richard E., Thaddeus W.B. Bligh, and Jessica F. Garden. "The Hebb Synapse Before Hebb: Theories of Synaptic Function in Learning and Memory Before Hebb (1949)." *Frontiers in Behavioral Neuroscience* 15 (October 2021). https://www.frontiersin.org/articles/10.3389/fnbeh.2021.732195/full

Hebb, Donald O. *The Organization of Behavior: A Neuropsychological Theory.* New York: Wiley. 1949.

Simpson, J.A., and E.S.C. Weiner, eds. *The Oxford English Dictionary.* 2nd ed. Oxford: Clarendon Press. 1989.

Chapter 9: Neurocognitive Architecture

Some Basic Neuroanatomy

What exactly *is* the brain?

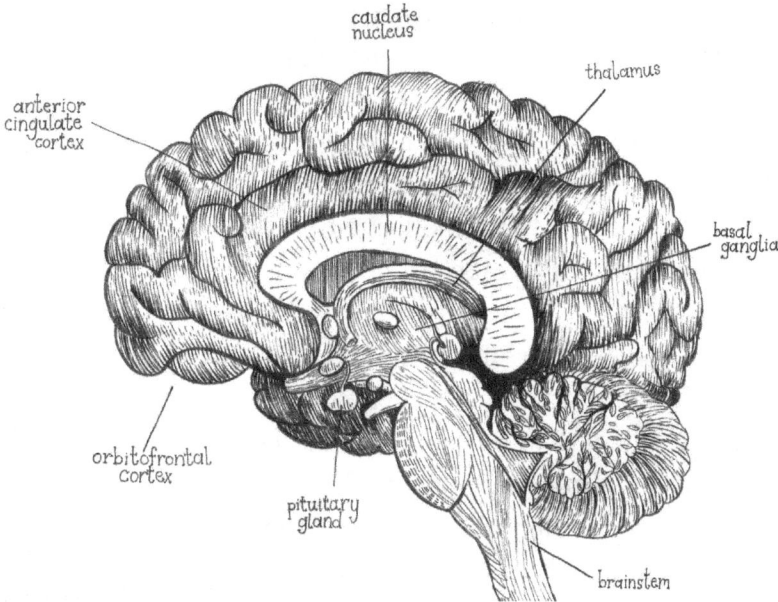

Figure 9.1

DOI: 10.4324/9781003626725-10

The Mastermind

So far, we've approached the brain on the micro level. Now we're going to take a step back and approach this subject on the macro level. The brain is the organ in the skull that is associated with a person's thoughts, memories, actions, behaviors, physical senses, imagination, emotions, and creativity. According to the *OED*, the brain integrates and coordinates "the activities of the nervous system, and [it is] the source of the advanced behavioural, emotional, and cognitive capabilities of humans and other mammals". The brain is divided into a larger frontal portion, which is called the cerebrum; a smaller back portion, which is called the cerebellum; and two connected right and left halves, which are called hemispheres. At the base, or the brainstem, the medulla oblongata connects the brain to the spinal cord. In addition to being an organ in the body, the term "brain" also refers to "the person in control, the directing intelligence, the mastermind".[1] Just as the brain is the seat of sensory and intellectual power, this term evokes an overall guiding presence.

The brain is wonderfully complex. This organ is central to the functioning of our bodies, to the expression of our individuality, and to our ability to recognize a shared sense of our common humanity. Because this organ both relates to, and influences, so many aspects of life, it is powerful to have some basic knowledge of neuroanatomy. Neuroanatomy is the study of the structures of the brain, how they are organized, and how they work together. The diagram appearing at the beginning of this chapter depicts a human brain in a vertical, cross-sectional view. The drawing's elegant, calligraphic lines are both precise and stylized. The structures of the brain associated with the intellect and with basic bodily functions are clearly labelled, as are the regions associated with anxiety and OCD. These areas include the following:

- The brain stem, which is associated with survival instincts and "fight or flight" responses. This part of the brain helps to regulate breathing and heart rate, among other vital functions.
- The prefrontal cortex of the cerebrum, which is associated with higher orders of thinking, such as communication, problem solving, and rational analysis.
- The thalamus, which is the area of the brain where messages are relayed between the cerebral cortex (or the outer layer of the brain) and the spinal cord. These messages include both sensory and motor signals. The thalamus helps to maintain our sense of alertness and to direct our attention accordingly.
- The orbitofrontal cortex, which helps to process sensory information relating to taste, touch, smell, sound, and sight. This part of the brain assesses the different qualities of incoming sensory information, and it integrates this knowledge with learning patterns relating to rewards, expectations, and decision-making abilities.[2]
- The cingulate cortex, which connects the emotional and thinking systems of the brain. This area is a kind of "connecting hub of emotions, sensations, and actions" relating to motivation, reward, memory, learning, and control, including impulse control.[3]

- The caudate nucleus, which is part of the striatum. This area helps us to plan the movements of our bodies, and it plays an important role in learning, memory processing, and visual information processing. The caudate nucleus is also involved in "reward, motivation, emotion, and romantic interaction".[4]
- The pituitary gland, which both produces, and plays an important role in releasing, many different types of hormones.[5] We will look more closely at this gland in Chapter 12.

Basic knowledge of neuroanatomy provides a foundation for understanding the architecture of the human brain and the different neural systems associated with thinking, emotions, actions, and behaviors. We will explore these subjects in detail in the upcoming chapters.

Exercise for Reflection and Journaling

You can practice identifying how different aspects of your brain function and how they relate to one another. This exercise can help you to hone your skills of observation and description. It may also provide you with greater clarity and detachment when approaching emotionally charged subjects and situations.

- Choose a subject that you love and that intrigues you. It can be anything at all. The subject can come from nature—such as an animal or a flower. Or it can come from sports or music, or from life experience, such as a favorite holiday or celebration. While I love all animals, I especially love cats, so I will use the example of a cat.

You may wish to choose a dog or a bird or a horse—or a soccer ball or a guitar—or an object from Christmas morning or from your birthday. The possibilities are endless, and the choices are deeply personal. The key is to select something vivid that you love and that you are fascinated by. Two or three sentences will suffice when responding to the following prompts.

- If you were to consider the example of a cat, you would begin by looking up the word "cat" in a dictionary, an encyclopedia, or another reference work. Make careful note of the definition, the subject's primary characteristics, and perhaps the history of the term. As you do this, you are working *intellectually and analytically*, and your frontal cortex is engaged.

- Now, go into bodily memory and recreate the sensory experience of engaging with this subject. How does it feel to pet your cat (or strum the guitar, or kick the soccer ball, or open a present, or eat a big slice of cherry pie with whipped cream)? Which bodily senses are engaged? How do you move your muscles, and how does your body respond in a coordinated way when you are performing these actions? Connect deeply with the memory of the experience and create the most vivid sensory description that you can. As you do this, you are working *kinesthetically*. Your caudate nucleus, frontal cortex, and cerebellum are all involved when performing the activity, as are other parts of your brain and spinal cord.

- Now, call up the subject in your mind once again and ask yourself how this subject feels emotionally. Allow yourself to feel pleasure, joy, and love as you contemplate the cat (or the soccer game, or holding the instrument and playing a song, or having a meal with your loved ones). What types of adjectives, colors, pictures, and symbols do you associate with your responses? As you do this, you are working *emotionally and affectively*, and your limbic system is engaged. We will examine this system in the next chapter.

- Now, re-read your sentences and notice what each perspective offers individually, and how they all work together to create the fullness of the experience. In this exercise, it's as though you are isolating and then integrating the various strands of your own neurocognitive experience. You are seeing the trees, the forest, and the connections that make these experiences possible. As you do this, you are consciously exploring the process of "knowing together"— cognition.

- Of all the concepts you've learned so far, which aspect of the brain intrigues you the most and why? How does the answer to this question provide insight into your own mind and inner character? What does this show you about yourself? As always, record your observations and descriptions in your journal.

Notes

1 See the entry on "brain" in the *OED*: https://www.oed.com/dictionary/brain_n?tab=meaning_and_use#15283926

The *OED* further notes that the brain consists "of soft grey or white tissue with . . . a conspicuously convoluted surface", as well as "the substance or tissue of this organ comprising nerve cells and nerve fibres".

2   Regarding the orbitofrontal cortex, see Edmund T. Rolls, "The Functions of the Orbitofrontal Cortex", *Brain Cognition* 55 (2004): https://pubmed.ncbi.nlm.nih.gov/15134840/ and Morten L. Kringelbach, "The Human Orbitofrontal Cortex: Linking Rewards to Hedonic Experience", *Nature Reviews Neuroscience* 6 (2005): https://www.nature.com/articles/nrn1747

3   Regarding the cingulate cortex, see Francis L. Stevens et al., "Anterior Cingulate Cortex: Unique Role in Cognition and Emotion", *Journal of Neuropsychiatry and Clinical Neurosciences* 23, no. 2 (April 2011): https://neuro.psychiatryonline.org/doi/10.1176/jnp.23.2.jnp121 and Fareed R. Jumah and Rimal H. Dossani, "Neuroanatomy: Cingulate Cortex", *StatPearls*, 2002: https://www.ncbi.nlm.nih.gov/books/NBK537077/

4   See Margaret E. Driscoll et al., "Neuroanatomy: Nucleus Caudate", *StatPearls*, 2023: https://www.ncbi.nlm.nih.gov/books/NBK557407/#:~:text=Introduction,in%20various%20higher%20neurological%20functions

5   For a general discussion of the pituitary gland, see "Anatomy of the Pituitary Gland": https://www.hopkinsmedicine.org/health/conditions-and-diseases/the-pituitary-gland

References

Driscoll, Margaret E., et al. "Neuroanatomy: Nucleus Caudate." *StatPearls,* 2023. https://www.ncbi.nlm.nih.gov/books/NBK557407/#:~:text=Introduction,in%20various%20higher%20neurological%20functions

Jumah, Fareed R., and Rimal H. Dossani. "Neuroanatomy: Cingulate Cortex." *StatPearls,* 2002. https://www.ncbi. nlm.nih.gov/books/NBK537077/

Kringelbach, Morten L. "The human orbitofrontal cortex: Linking rewards to hedonic experience." *Nature Reviews Neuroscience* 6 (2005). https://www.nature. com/articles/nrn1747

Rolls, Edmund T. "The Functions of the Orbitofrontal Cortex." *Brain Cognition* 55 (2004). https://pubmed. ncbi.nlm.nih.gov/15134840/

Simpson, J.A., and E.S.C. Weiner, eds. *The Oxford English Dictionary*. 2nd ed. Oxford: Clarendon Press. 1989.

Stevens, Francis L., Robin A. Hurley, and Katherine H. Taber. "Anterior Cingulate Cortex: Unique Role in Cognition and Emotion." *Journal of Neuropsychiatry and Clinical Neurosciences* 23, no. 2 (April 2011). https://neuro.psychiatryonline.org/doi/10.1176/ jnp.23.2.jnp121

Chapter 10: A Party in the Mansion

The Limbic System

Human beings love a good story, and our stories are rich in analogies and visual metaphors.

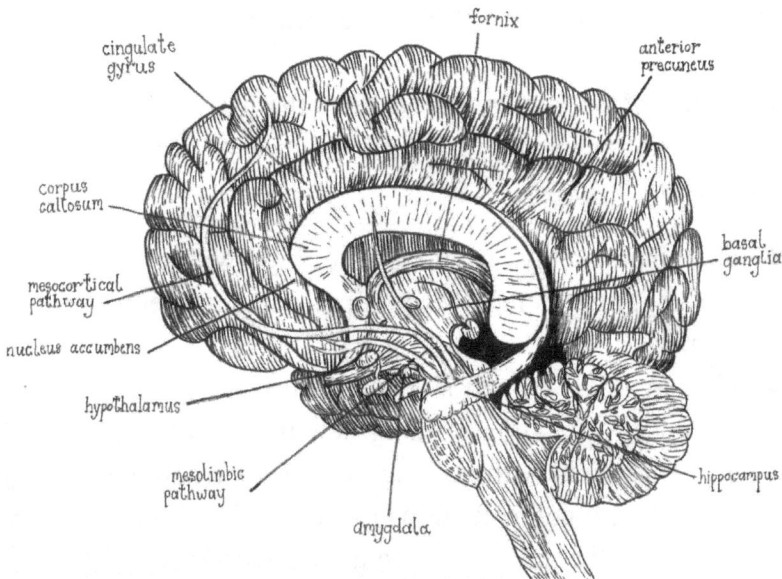

Figure 10.1

DOI: 10.4324/9781003626725-11

The Anatomy of Emotion

Within the brain, the limbic system is associated with memory, emotion, behavior, motivation, thinking, learning, pleasure, and survival. The limbic system is located above the brainstem and beneath the cerebral cortex, which is the outermost part of the brain.[1] The name of this system refers to the limbic lobe of the cerebrum, which has "the character of a border", and which has been described as "a mechanism for emotion".[2] The word "limbic" also relates to "limb"—like the limb of a body or the limb of a tree. In this illustration, the crinkled folds of the cerebellum, which is located at the very back of the skull, behind the hippocampus, resemble the stylized leaves of a trailing vine.

This elegant line drawing illustrates the basic anatomical structures associated with the limbic system, which include the following:

- The hippocampus, which is associated with emotions, learning, and memory, including spatial and emotional memories.
- The amygdala, which is associated with emotional responses, including forming new memories and investing them with varying degrees of emotional strength and color. Regions of the hippocampus, and especially the amygdala, are associated with strong emotional memories, and with experiences that are more likely to be remembered than those associated with more neutral events.[3]
- The hypothalamus, which helps to maintain homeostasis, or steadiness and stability, in various bodily

systems—including those associated with hunger, thirst, temperature, blood pressure, etc.

- The cingulate gyrus, which helps to regulate behaviors and emotions, particularly those associated with pain and fear. This area also links sight and smell with emotional memory.
- The basal ganglia, which helps to control body posture, balance, and voluntary movements, such as eye movements. Within the basal ganglia, the nucleus accumbens is associated with desire and emotional reinforcement, and with habit formation and addiction.
- The mesolimbic pathway, which transports the neurotransmitter dopamine to the nucleus accumbens and to the amygdala. These structures are associated with thinking and motivation, particularly relating to rewards, goals, and incentives.[4] In this illustration, the branching forms of the mesolimbic pathway imaginatively resemble the tendrils of a curling root or vine.

Why We Love Metaphors

Neuroscientists have shown that when people engage with creative visual metaphors and poetic analogies, the brain's limbic system is activated to trigger a reward response.[5] In a pioneering study of 1999, the researcher V.S. Ramachandran studied how the human brain responds to works of visual art. He examined the different qualities that people find attractive when looking at pictures, and he identified a corresponding series of underlying categories and patterns. Ramachandran also made an important discovery that helped to shape the field of descriptive neuroaesthetics. As he observed, "a metaphor is a mental tunnel between two concepts or percepts that appear grossly dissimilar on the surface". While grasping analogies is important for communication, learning, and survival, the

> discovery of similarities and the linking of superficially dissimilar events would lead to a limbic activation—in order to ensure that the process is rewarding. It is this basic mechanism that one taps into, whether with puns, poetry, or visual art.[6]

Within the course of evolutionary biology,
The human brain has been developed by stories
That are full of symbols and rich in analogies.
Our stories are like our mirrors.
They help us to know who we are,
How we relate to the world,
What we like,
And what we don't like.
All our lives, for years and years,
We sit around waiting for a good story.
And then, one finally comes . . .

Our stories give us a sense of validation,
Of joy and pleasure, of sadness and fear.
Our stories give us all the wonderful emotions that we get to have
Because we live in bodies with complex brains and active limbic systems.

If we were to approach these themes through the metaphorical lens of deer trails through the woods, we would see the similarities between the history of the limbic system and the history of the forest:

Ones who know how
Can walk into a forest and see its history:
How long it's been there.
When a logger came through.
When an ice storm came through.
When a great shift in the weather came through.
Ones who know how can go in and read a forest.

In the human body, the limbic system can be seen as a place
Where the human condition resides:
In its stories,
In the history of its glory,
And the history of its deep understanding,
Of language, connection, and unity.

One day, those who know how
Will be able to go in and read the limbic system
And see the development of a human being:
When language came online for a person,
Through the recognition of sound.
When joy came online,
Through metaphor and play.
When understanding came online,
Through connection to family.
Those who know how to read these structures will be
able to see
The first time a person recognized their mother, father,
grandmother, or grandfather.
They will even be able to see

When a person's connection to their own humanity came online,
And they became aware of their connection to the humanity of others,
And to a greater sense of humanity itself.

Human beings have so many layers. No one fully knows them all, because we don't yet have the technology to see all the layers and map them precisely. We do know that some of the deepest and oldest limbic system responses are formed when a child first recognizes the love of its family. Not surprisingly, these themes also arise when I work with people at the end of life. It's like a joining of last and first things. One older man told me that he loved his family because "family is where the first experiences of love come from". While relationships change over time, and they go through many difficulties and challenges, "family is the first experience of love".

A Party in the Mansion

If we were to create a visual metaphor for an engaged limbic system, we might picture a party in the mansion of the brain.

In this illustration, the mansion is draped with festive garlands that resemble the curling trails of the mesolimbic pathway. Each window is brightly illuminated, as if opening onto a room with its own light switch, and which holds its own story. When you experience the pleasures of visual art, poetry, theater, cinema, music, or literature,

Figure 10.2

you can always think of your limbic system and medial orbitofrontal cortex lighting up, in response. This may feel like pure joy—or like a party in the mansion of your brain.

Exercise for Reflection and Journaling

This discussion of the limbic system invites you to consider your own preferences, joys, and what lights you up from within:

- What kinds of stories do you love?
- What kinds of images do you love?
- What kinds of music do you love?
- What do these art forms have in common? Do you recognize common themes or patterns among them?

- How are these art forms different? In their differences, how do they offer novel opportunities for neurocognitive insights, or for the art of "knowing together"?
- Have you ever looked in the mirror and seen your own face light up when you hear such stories, or look at such pictures, or listen to such music?
- If you were to plan a really great party around these themes, what kinds of images and colors would you use for your motifs and decorations?
- What do these questions show you about the relationships between thought, pleasure, and emotion? As always, record your observations and descriptions in your journal. You may surprise yourself by your own creativity, and how your creativity is linked to your own intelligence.

Notes

1 For a general discussion of the limbic system, see Sanat Pai Raikar, "Limbic System", *Encyclopaedia Britannica*: https://www.britannica.com/science/limbic-system

2 The word "limbic" derives from the Latin *limbus*, which refers to a border, hem, edge, or fringe. See the entry in the *OED*: https://www.oed.com/dictionary/limbic_adj?tab=meaning_and_use#39187241

3 J. Hogeveen, C. Salvi, and J. Grafman, "Emotional Intelligence: Lessons from Lesions", *Trends in Neurosciences* 39, no. 10 (October 2016), 699.

4 According to the *OED*, the mesolimbic pathway is "a neuronal pathway that originates in the mesencephalon

and projects to the limbic system". This region acts as a signaling center that controls dopamine release and uptake, and it helps to regulate addictive behaviors. Regarding the structures and functions of the mesolimbic pathway, see Antonio Alcaro et al., "Behavioral Functions of the Mesolimbic Dopaminergic System: An Affective Neuroethological Perspective", *Brain Research Review* 56 (December 2007): https://www.ncbi.nlm.nih.gov/pmc/articles/PMC2238694/

5 See Faith A. Pak and Ethan B. Reichsman, "Beauty and the Brain: The Emerging Field of Neuroaesthetics", *The Harvard Crimson* (November 10, 2017): https://www.thecrimson.com/article/2017/11/10/neuroaesthetics-cover/

6 V.S. Ramachandran and William Hirstein, "The Science of Art: A Neurological Theory of Aesthetic Experience", *Journal of Consciousness Studies* 6, no. 6–7 (1999): https://philpapers.org/archive/RAMTSO-5.pdf. Ramachandran further supported his argument by citing work with patients suffering from the neurological disorder Capgras syndrome, a condition that is characterized by "the absence of limbic activation". As Ramachandran noted, in Capgras patients the

connections for the visual "face region" in the inferotemporal cortex to the amygdala (a part of the limbic system where activation leads to emotions) are severed so that a familiar face no longer evokes a warm fuzzy emotional response.

Such patients are thus unable to link multiple views of a person's face, or to recognize that the face belongs to a single person, rather than to multiple individuals.

References

Alcaro, Antonio, Robert Huber, and Jaak Panksepp. "Behavioral Functions of the Mesolimbic Dopaminergic System: An Affective Neuroethological Perspective." *Brain Research Review* 56 (December 2007). https://www.ncbi.nlm.nih.gov/pmc/articles/PMC2238694/

Hogeveen, J., C. Salvi, and J. Grafman. "Emotional Intelligence: Lessons from Lesions." *Trends in Neurosciences* 39, no. 10 (October 2016).

Pak, Faith A., and Ethan B. Reichsman. "Beauty and the Brain: The Emerging Field of Neuroaesthetics." *The Harvard Crimson,* November 10, 2017. https://www.thecrimson.com/article/2017/11/10/neuroaesthetics-cover/

Raikar, Sanat Pai. "Limbic System." *Encyclopaedia Britannica.* https://www.britannica.com/science/limbic-system

Ramachandran, V.S., and William Hirstein. "The Science of Art: A Neurological Theory of Aesthetic Experience." *Journal of Consciousness Studies* 6, no. 6–7 (1999): 15–51. https://web.archive.org/web/20120302011954/http://www.imprint.co.uk/rama/art.pdf

Simpson, J.A., and E.S.C. Weiner, eds. *The Oxford English Dictionary*. 2nd ed. Oxford: Clarendon Press. 1989.

Chapter 11: Like a Shiny Silver Antenna

Empathy and the Anterior Precuneus

What if I told you that inside your brain, you have something like a shiny silver antenna that processes subtle energy and information?

Figure 11.1

DOI: 10.4324/9781003626725-12

An Inner Antenna

Can you feel your limbic system lighting up as you consider this intriguing possibility? One of the most fascinating ways that human beings process subtle information involves an area of the brain called the anterior precuneus. This region is located toward the back of the skull, in the parietal lobe, above the cerebellum. In this watercolor, the anterior precuneus is located where the shiny silver antenna attaches to the roof of the nearest tower (see also *Figure 10.1*).

The anterior precuneus is associated with both visual and mental imagery, as well as with issues relating to human consciousness and self-reflection.[1] Neuroaesthetic studies have shown that the anterior precuneus plays "a pivotal role in mental imagery of high self-relevance, [which] might be driven by the scenario visualizations that are known to be particularly vivid for highly emotional moments. The anterior precuneus has also been associated with the ability to switch one's perspective from self-reference to the content of other people's minds, and with judgments requiring empathy".[2] Researchers have also discovered that the precuneus region becomes activated when people are immersed in feelings of love.[3]

Why Empathy Matters So Deeply

Let's consider the subject of empathy. Empathy is the ability to sense another person's feelings, thoughts, or ideas. This quality can allow you to relate to other people with great compassion and intimacy. Empathy can also be a strategy for coping and survival. When a person lives in a threatening environment, knowing the rules of the environment may be equated with feelings of safety. A small child may look around and notice that their home is not such a safe or stable place to be, and this can be very frightening. The child may think that if they can just figure out the rules, then they will know what is safe and what is not, and that this knowledge may protect them from harm. The child may also see that when a person stops playing by the rules, bad things can happen. Then the child may observe the world around them very carefully to understand how the rules play out from moment to moment. They may study the facial expressions and subtle emotional energies that emanate from authority figures, so that they can morph and adjust as different situations arise.

In some people, the empathic part of the brain
May be a little more developed and finely tuned than in others.
This involves both nature and nurture.
A person can be born with this area of the brain
A little bit more finely tuned,
But if they are born into an environment
Where such fine-tuning is not necessary for survival,
This ability may not develop very much.

But, if you take a little bit of fine tuning,
And you place a baby into a situation
Where emotional attunement to its environment brings it safety,
Then that place in the brain is going to become more heightened,

Because the child soon realizes:
"Oh, I must reach out and look around,
And feel other people's feelings,
So that I can adjust my behavior to feel safe here".
This is nature, and it is nurture.

Empathy can be a two-sided coin.
If this quality is used wisely,
Empathy has great rewards.
It can help us, not only with survival,
But with feeling a deep connection to other human
beings,
To nature, and to the beauty of life itself.
That can feel like pure bliss.

Empathy can also be a detriment if not used wisely.
An empathic person can learn to see and feel,
Not just the light of the world,
But the darkness around a person or place.
Then they may feel completely overwhelmed
By another person's fear,
By their anxiety, or their aggression.
There can be a moment
When a person is embracing nature in an empathic way,
And that is a beautiful, uplifting moment.
But when that person is in their home and someone walks
in the door,
And they can feel their anger,
It does not feel very good.

This is why empathy can feel like a blessing, or like a curse.
Empathy can heighten joy,

And it can also heighten anxiety.
The balance is always available,
Even if it is not always taken.

The Balance Is Always Available

Sometimes a person's level of empathy is not in balance.
Some individuals feel too much empathy, while others don't
feel enough. Both conditions involve boundary issues, and
both need work. If a person is overly empathetic, then they
may have very poor boundaries. If a person absorbs too
much energy from their surroundings, they can become
weakened and drained. Yet if a person is underly sensitized
to others and to their environment, then life can be very
difficult for the people around them. When someone is overly
empathetic—they know it. The person can feel it, and their
own sensitivity tells them that it is so. But when someone
is insufficiently empathetic, then they usually don't know it.
While the person might get the message from those around
them, ultimately, it is up to them to be more sensitive. In all
cases, greater awareness can lead to greater balance.

Silver Is Both a Great Conductor and a Great Reflector

Within the brain, the anterior precuneus is like a shiny
silver antenna
Reaching out and reading the world.
You can envision the world all around you
As sending energy and information to this inner antenna.

Silver is a great conductor, and it is also a great reflector.
This precious metal moves energy quickly and clearly,
without obstruction.
Silver is a bit of a mirror whose surface can reflect
anything in its field.
Just as the anterior precuneus is like an antenna,
The stories it reflects are like mirrors.

They help us to know who we are,
And how we relate to the world,
Both inside and out.

Sometimes life is beautiful and glorious. And sometimes life is extremely difficult. These metaphorical images can help you to hold yourself true and bright, no matter what arises, and no matter what is received or reflected.

Exercise for Reflection and Journaling

As we have seen, too much empathy and too little empathy both involve boundary issues, and both conditions need work. This exercise can help you to cultivate the tools of self-awareness and recognition:

- Think of a subject that moves you very deeply and that is close to your heart—but one that is not your own. This can be a challenging situation that involves other people or a larger cause in the world. The cause could relate to the environment or to social justice—or it could relate to a difficult situation that someone you know has recently experienced.

- With the example clearly in mind, imagine how it would feel to over-empathize with another person's situation. What would happen if you identified so deeply that you made this issue your own rather than the other person's? Would you quickly become exhausted and drained? Would you still be able to be a good friend and have an effective presence? At what point would your own distress blot out the other person's experiences and responses so that the issue became all about you and your feelings rather than being about them and their feelings? Make careful notes in your journal about the condition of over-empathizing.

- Now, imagine under-empathizing with the same person or situation. What would happen if your perspective was so callous and your boundaries were so hard that you became indifferent to those around you? What if your first thought was always, "Well, that's a tough situation, but that's **their problem, not mine!** This has absolutely nothing to do with me!" How would that feel? Would it be pleasant for others to be around you, or even, for you to be around yourself? Again, make careful notes in your journal about what you see and feel from the perspective of under-empathizing.

- Now, imagine approaching the same person or situation with a sense of balance. How does *that* feel? How close is this approach to your own familiar practice? If you see a differential, consider the types of adjustments that you may wish to make in your thinking.

- As always, make careful notes in your journal. This comparative perspective is very powerful because it cultivates the kind of balance that can lead to wisdom.

Notes

1 Regarding the precuneus region of the brain, see Andrea E. Cavanna and Michael R. Trimble, "The Precuneus: A Review of Its Functional Anatomy and Behavioural Correlates", *Brain* 129, no. 3 (March 2006): https://pubmed.ncbi.nlm.nih.gov/16399806/

2 As quoted in Eugen Wassiliwizky et al., "The Emotional Power of Poetry: Neural Circuitry, Psychophysiology and Compositional Principles", *Social Cognitive and Affective Neuroscience* 12, no. 8 (August 2017): 1229–1240: https://www.researchgate.net/publication/316630388_The_emotional_power_of_poetry_neural_circuitry_ps. Regarding these subjects, G. Gabrielle Starr has observed that "two components of the default mode network, the temporoparietal junction and the medial prefrontal cortex, are involved in theory of mind—the simulation of others' consciousness and the imputation of inner life to them". See G. Gabrielle Starr, *Feeling Beauty: The Neuroscience of Aesthetic Experience* (Cambridge, MA: MIT Press, 2015), 60. Other researchers have concluded that the neural mechanisms associated with empathy remain unclear: "Because the perception–action model relies on distributed representations created online, in the moment, to capture a target's state and situation, empathy is not necessarily associated with any one neural 'empathy area' or even 'empathy circuit'. It does not even necessarily involve single-cell mirror neurons or even 'empathic' brain areas like the insula or the anterior cingulate. Indeed, according to the strong cognitive science perception-action view, it almost

does not make sense to write. . .about the neural bases of empathy, because the neural correlate in any given situation includes a large, distributed representation that is necessary to encapsulate that specific event and that changes depending on the nature of the event or task". See Stephanie D. Preston, "Neural and Physiological Mechanisms of Altruism and Empathy," in *The Oxford Handbook of Positive Psychology*, 3rd ed., eds. C. R. Snyder, Shane J. Lopez, Lisa M. Edwards, and Susana Marques. (Oxford University Press, 2021), Chapter 53.

3 See Pärttyli Rinne et al., "Six Types of Love Differentially Recruit Reward and Social Cognition Brain Areas", *Cerebral Cortex* 34, no. 8 (August 2024): https://pubmed.ncbi.nlm.nih.gov/39183646/

References

Cavanna, Andrea E., and Michael R. Trimble. "The Precuneus: A Review of its Functional Anatomy and Behavioural Correlates." *Brain* 129, no. 3 (March 2006). https://pubmed.ncbi.nlm.nih.gov/16399806/

Preston, Stephanie D. "Neural and Physiological Mechanisms of Altruism and Empathy." In *The Oxford Handbook of Positive Psychology*. 3rd ed., edited by C.R. Snyder, Shane J. Lopez, Lisa M. Edwards, and Susana Marques. New York: Oxford University Press. 2021.

Rinne, Pärttyli, Juha M. Lahnakoski, Heini Saarimäki, Mikke Tavast, Mikko Sams, and Linda Henriksson, "Six Types of Love Differentially Recruit Reward and Social Cognition Brain Areas." *Cerebral Cortex* 34, no. 8 (August 2024). https://pubmed.ncbi.nlm.nih.gov/39183646/

Starr, G. Gabrielle. *Feeling Beauty: The Neuroscience of Aesthetic Experience.* Cambridge, MA: MIT Press. 2015.

Wassiliwizky, Eugen, Stefan Koelsch, Valentin Wagner, Thomas Jacobsen, and Winfried Menninghaus. "The Emotional Power of Poetry: Neural Circuitry, Psychophysiology and Compositional Principles." *Social Cognitive and Affective Neuroscience* 12, no. 8 (August 2017): 1229–1240. https://www.researchgate. net/publication/316630388_The_emotional_power_of_ poetry_neural_circuitry_ps

Chapter 12: Connections Light Connections

Intuition, the Pituitary Gland, and the Prefrontal Cortex

The pituitary gland is a master gland. It is both a great translator, and a great transmitter, of information.

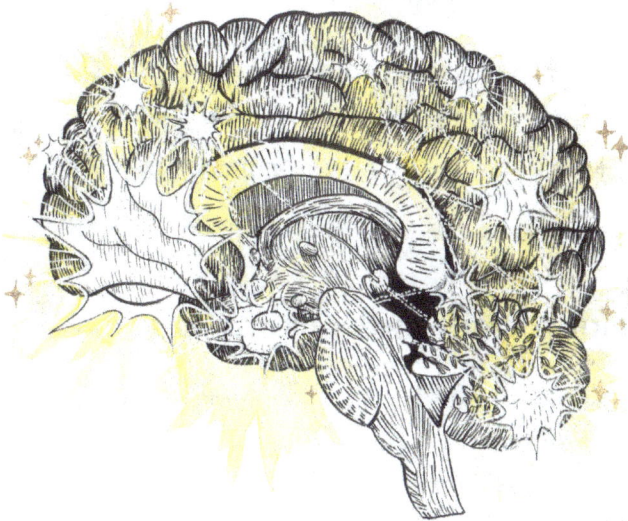

Figure 12.1

DOI: 10.4324/9781003626725-13

The Great Translator: The Pituitary Gland

The pituitary gland is a small neuroendocrine gland that plays "an important role in endocrine regulation and the control of growth, development, and metabolism".[1] This gland sits at the center of the brain, behind the eyes and ears. It is the size of a pea, and it consists of two lobes and a stalk. The pituitary gland produces many important hormones, and it regulates the secretion of hormones into the bloodstream by "carrying messages . . . to various organs, skin, muscles, and other tissues".

The root of the word "hormone" means "to set in motion". Hormones are chemical compounds that regulate the activities of cells, including those associated with growth, reproduction, metabolism, and stress responses.[2] Through both nerves and blood vessels, the pituitary stalk connects the pituitary gland to the hypothalamus. This region of the brain sends messages to the nervous system to control functions such as heart rate, blood pressure, and breathing.[3] These activities can become pronounced in highly charged situations.

Blocking and Unblocking Our Own Light

The pituitary gland is a master gland
That both receives and sends messages.
It is like a beacon.
There is a call and a response.
When information comes into the brain,

*The pituitary gland already has all of the languages that
it needs
To translate the information instantly.*

*Yet when a person is experiencing severe anxiety and OCD,
All of the information may not be getting through.
It's as though the person's energy has been diminished,
And their light has been dimmed.
The light is still there.
But it's like it has been placed in a too-tight shell,
With a hardened outer layer.*

*As a person heals and transforms,
Then the shell cracks and disintegrates,
The way a snake sheds its skin.
Then the light can shine more fully and freely,
Both in the body, and in the life.*

The Anatomy of Illumination

The illustration appearing at the beginning of this chapter
shows the human brain in a state of illumination. In
the drawing, the brain appears to be both subtle and
monumental, complex and magical. Amidst the intricate
calligraphic linework, radiant golden and white light
appear to emanate from the pituitary gland and the
prefrontal cortex. The prefrontal cortex is the lobe that
sits at the front of the brain, directly behind the forehead.
This anatomical drawing has a visionary quality. The
golden sparkles within and around the brain evoke both
the flashes of neuronal firing and glimmers of epiphanic
insight.

In moments of inspiration and connection,
The pituitary gland lights up,
And it begins to communicate throughout the brain
And down into the nervous system.

When you are walking a path of transformation,
You are not disregarding your body,
Your brain, or your heart.
You are not disregarding your connections
To the world all around you.

As you come to understand these connections even more
deeply,
You can imagine your pituitary gland and prefrontal
cortex
Lighting up with pure white light,
Just as artists have pictured images of illumination
For hundreds and hundreds of years.

Throughout history, when painters and sculptors have sought to depict enlightened individuals, they often place haloes of golden-white light around their head. It's as though the prefrontal cortex is lighting up from within. Haloes are symbols that translate subtle energy into clear visual metaphors that the mind can easily grasp. For centuries, this golden-white light has served as a metaphor for visionary consciousness. At the same time, absolutely everyone has experienced such powerful moments of inspiration, illumination, and joy. Many people also have a strong sense of intuition. The term "intuition" means to look inward, to contemplate what is seen, and to reflect on the insights that arise.[4]

Intuition: Lining Up and Lighting Up

Just as information is communicated instantly in the
world all around us, subtle processes of communication
immediately unfold in our brain and mind, as well.

When a person's brain and mind say:
"I want to do something . . ."
The brain checks in with the heart.
When the heart says, "Yes",
It's like the brain and the mind become more elevated.
It's like the person begins to receive more energy,
And they begin to transmit more energy.
It's like there is more light inside of them.
When the brain and the heart are in alignment,
Things can get very big.
A tremendous amount of energy can flow through the
system because,
When we line up, we light up.

When the mind says, "I want to do this!",
And the heart says, "No, no, don't do that!"
And the mind says, "Well, I'm going to do it
anyway . . ."
Then everything is out of joint.
It can feel like ideas and actions are coming from a
lower place.
Sometimes it can feel like these disruptive energies
Are like an army of horsemen riding in on egos,
And they can get into a mob mentality pretty quickly.
When this happens, you can feel the energy in
the air.

When the heart and the mind line up and light up,
Then there is a larger sense of alignment,
And you can feel this, as well.
It has a magnetism to it.
You might say to yourself,
"Oh, I like what that person is doing, or thinking, or
making.
I can't help it.
I'm magnetized by it".

Connections light connections,
Both within and around us,
Because when we line up,
We light up.

Exercise for Reflection and Journaling

Learning how to read subtle networks of energy is
a powerful intuitive skill. When you do this, you
are actively working with the light of your own
consciousness. When you disregard this information, you
are working against yourself, and that is a battle that no
one can win. As you practice your intuitive skills, you can
see where you are blocking your own light. To become
acquainted with your own sense of intuition, reflect on the
following scenarios:

- Imagine that you have just heard about a new
  opportunity and that you immediately feel it is
  something that you want to try. You just know it without
  even thinking about it. Maybe it is a challenging class
  that you want to take, or a creative activity that you

want to learn. As you hear about the opportunity, your inner pathways light up. How would you describe this feeling, both in your mind and in your body? Record your thoughts and observations carefully in your journal, and consider the following:

- Imagine signing up for the activity, even if you had to push yourself to get started. After a few sessions you might love it, and a new world opens up for you. How does that make you feel? Even if you discover that this activity is not what you expected, or that it is ultimately not the right thing for you, you are still grateful for having had the experience and proud of yourself for giving it a try. In these scenarios, you worked with your own intuition. How does this make you feel, both in your mind and in your body?

- Now, imagine that the same opportunity arises, but this time you don't go for it. You might be too intimidated, or you might be lazy and let the deadline slip by. Or you might lack confidence and tell yourself that you can only fail at this, so why even bother? As these thoughts arise, you listen to them, even though another part of your mind urges you to try the activity, anyway. How do these competing thoughts make you feel, both in your mind and in your body?

- Now imagine that you tried the activity, and that you disliked it. Yet even after you discovered that this was not for you, you kept forcing yourself to go, out of habit, pride, stubbornness, or the embarrassment of looking like a quitter. How are you working against your own intuition? How do these thoughts make you feel, both in your mind and in your body?

- Why is it powerful to be able to recognize your own intuitive responses clearly and consciously, both in your mind and in your body? Why is it powerful to find language to describe your responses, and to see how they map onto larger patterns of thought and behavior? Intuition is often very subtle, which is why careful observation and description are such powerful tools when cultivating this important skill.

Notes

1 See the entry on the "pituitary gland" in the *OED*: https://www.oed.com/dictionary/pituitary-gland_n?tab=meaning_and_use#29887876100

2 A hormone is "any of numerous organic compounds that are secreted into the body fluids of an animal, particularly the bloodstream, by a specific group of cells and regulate some specific physiological activity of other cells; (also) any synthetic compound having such an effect". See the entries on "hormone" in the *OED*: https://www.oed.com/dictionary/hormone_n?tab=meaning_and_use&hide-all-quotations=true#1267123 and https://www.oed.com/dictionary/hormone_n?tab=etymology&hide-all-quotations=true#1267123

3 For an overall discussion of the pituitary gland, see: https://my.clevelandclinic.org/health/body/21459-pituitary-gland

4 See the entry on "intuition" in the *OED:* https://www.
   oed.com/dictionary/intuition_n?tab=meaning_and_
   use&hide-all-quotations=true#167187

References

Simpson, J.A., and E.S.C. Weiner, eds. *The Oxford English Dictionary*. 2nd ed. Oxford: Clarendon Press. 1989.

Part II: The Art of Holding On by Letting Go

Reenvisioning Anxiety and OCD

Chapter 13: Life Is Not Always a Party

The Brain, Anxiety, and OCD

Life is not always a party.

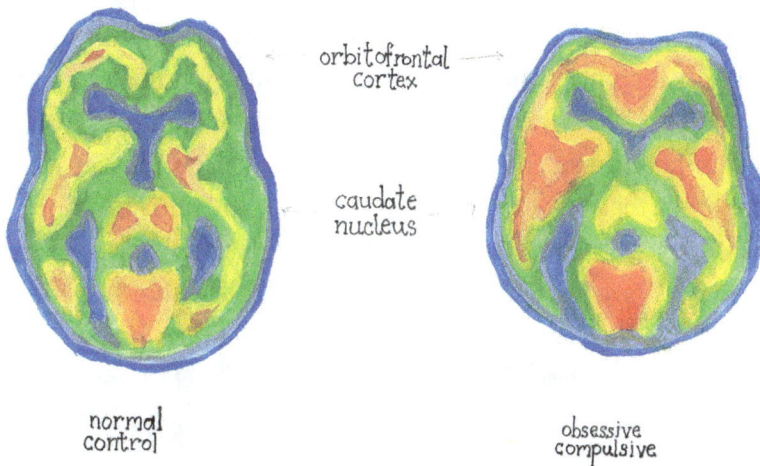

Figure 13.1

DOI: 10.4324/9781003626725-15

Visualizing Patterns of Disruption

Just as the brain's limbic system lights up when a person experiences pleasure and joy, so too does this system become activated in times of stress and anxiety. Anxiety is a severe form of worry or unease. This feeling can arise when a person is troubled about something, and it can become particularly intense when uncertainty is involved. Sometimes we fear that something *could* happen. Sometimes we worry that something *will* happen. And sometimes we dread that something *won't* happen.

The limbic system is associated with emotional processing and response. Within this system, the amygdala helps to process memories and emotions, particularly those relating to anxiety, fear, and aggression. If the amygdala perceives a significant threat, then it sends signals to the regions of the brain that can trigger the release of adrenalin into the bloodstream. A person may then experience tightness in the chest or stomach, tensing of the muscles, shortness of breath, racing heartbeat (tachycardia), sweating, and an overall sense of restlessness.

As I said, life is not always a party. . . .

Obsessions and Compulsions

Obsessive-compulsive disorder (OCD) is an anxiety disorder that consists of two primary components: obsessions, which are patterns of disturbing, unwanted thoughts or distressing images; and compulsions, which are the corresponding impulses to repeatedly perform actions to ease the worries or allay the disruptive thoughts.[1] According to the *Oxford English Dictionary*, an obsession is "a recurrent, intrusive, inappropriate thought, impulse, or image causing significant distress or disturbance to social or occupational functioning".[2] Common OCD patterns relate to issues concerning control, safety, or contamination. Thus, a person may line up objects rigidly in a row, or they may repeatedly check the locks of their house or scrub their hands—even when they *know* that things are in good order, that their home is secure, and that their hands are clean. Despite consciously recognizing that everything is fine, the person still experiences the disruptive thoughts and corresponding urges to act on the related impulses.

OCD often manifests during the teenage years. While anxiety can be present earlier, younger children tend to be more malleable in their relationship to the world.[3] The frontal cortex of the brain develops primarily during adolescence, between the ages of 12 and 25. The experiences that occur during this time are fundamental for cognitive development, including for the organization of thought and the patterning of behavior. When physical, mental, or emotional trauma are present, there can be a corresponding disruption in the development and organization of the prefrontal cortex.

In Part One, we learned that the orbitofrontal cortex helps to process sensory information relating to taste, touch, smell, sound, and sight. This area of the brain is associated with assessing the different values and qualities of this sensory information, and with integrating this knowledge into patterns associated with rewards, expectations, and decision-making.[4] We also saw that the caudate nucleus is the region of the brain surrounding the limbic system. The caudate nucleus helps us to plan the movements of our bodies, and it plays an important role in learning, emotional response, memory processing, and visual information processing.[5] These regions are all associated with processing strong emotions, integrating relevant information, and performing corresponding behaviors.

The Spinning Hamster Wheel

Adolescence is a time of transition when a person moves from childhood to adulthood. During adolescence, a person with OCD may have experienced some sort of trauma. As a child becomes a teenager, others may start to treat them differently. Sometimes when an adult sees that a child is no longer a child, they may become verbally or physically aggressive. The young person may not quite know how to respond, as their prefrontal cortex is still developing and organizing itself in relation to the world. When disruption occurs on the physical, mental, or emotional levels, the organization of the prefrontal cortex can become disrupted, and it can get stuck. When the brain gets stuck, it begins to loop and repeat as it tries to rewire correctly. The looping can become like a hamster spinning in its wheel.

Brain scans of individuals with OCD show patterns of heightened activity in the orbitofrontal cortex and the caudate nucleus. The watercolor at the beginning of this chapter depicts comparative images of "normal" brain function in a control subject (left) and the areas of the brain that are activated in a person with OCD (right). This drawing presents a stylized version of the type of imagery seen in clinical brain studies using PET (positron emission tomography) technology.[6] In these scans, the "hot" areas of the brain appear in red and orange, which indicate heightened levels of blood flow and metabolism. The scans show where the brain is hard at work, and where it is overworking.

Sometimes life can feel overwhelming. Things can pile up, the mind starts racing, and severe anxiety can come in. Sometimes when a person is feeling frightened or overwhelmed, the nervous system can go into a panic attack. A panic attack is like the nervous system attempting to reset itself, to get rid of a lot of energy very quickly, so that it can readjust. Things hit a crescendo in the system, and then there is a sense of frenzy, and then the system collapses so that it can go into a regenerative mode.

In the next chapter, we will explore how these themes relate to the imagery of the natural landscape, and how they can be translated into a neurocognitive fairytale about deer trails through the woods.

Exercise for Reflection and Journaling

- What are your hopes and goals as you read the next chapters of this book?

- How is reading this book an act of self-care?
- Record your thoughts and observations carefully in your journal. You will be prompted to return to this journal entry once you have reached the end of this section, following Chapter 21. You will then have gained a comparative perspective that will enable you to see what you have learned, and if your thinking has shifted.

Notes

1 For a general discussion of "Obsessive-Compulsive and Related Disorders", see: https://med.stanford.edu/ocd/about/understanding.html

2 See the definition of "obsession" in the *OED*: https://www.oed.com/dictionary/obsession_n?tab=meaning_and_use#34134708

3 Psychiatrists note that anxiety and OCD are known to peak during "late childhood/early adolescence and again in early adulthood". See Sanil Rege, "Obsessive-Compulsive Disorder (OCD): A Primer on Neurobiology, Diagnosis, and Treatment" (2018): https://psychscene.com/wp-content/uploads/2018/10/Obsessive-Compulsive-Disorder.pdf

4 Regarding the orbitofrontal cortex, see Edmund T. Rolls, "The Functions of the Orbitofrontal Cortex", *Brain Cognition* 55 (2004): https://pubmed.ncbi.nlm.nih.gov/15134840/ and Morten L. Kringelbach, "The Human Orbitofrontal Cortex: Linking Rewards to Hedonic Experience", *Nature Reviews Neuroscience* 6 (2005): https://www.nature.com/articles/nrn1747

5 See Margaret E. Driscoll et al., "Neuroanatomy: Nucleus Caudate", *StatPearls,* 2023: https://www.

ncbi.nlm.nih.gov/books/NBK557407/#:~:text=Introd
uction,in%20various%20higher%20neurological%20
functions

6 For a historically influential example of this type of
   imagery, see Lewis R. Baxter, Jr. et al., "Local Cerebral
   Glucose Metabolic Rates in Obsessive-Compulsive
   Disorder: A Comparison with Rates in Unipolar
   Depression and in Normal Controls", *Archives of
   General Psychiatry* 44 (March 1987): 211–218.

References

Baxter, Lewis R., Jr., Michael E. Phelps, and John C.
   Mazziotta. "Local Cerebral Glucose Metabolic Rates
   in Obsessive-Compulsive Disorder: A Comparison with
   Rates in Unipolar Depression and in Normal Controls."
   Archives of General Psychiatry 44 (March 1987):
   211–218.

Driscoll, Margaret E., Pradeep C. Bollu, and Prasanna
   Tadi. "Neuroanatomy: Nucleus Caudate." *StatPearls,*
   2023. https://www.ncbi.nlm.nih.gov/books/NBK5574
   07/#:~:text=Introduction,in%20various%20higher%20
   neurological%20functions

Kringelbach, Morten L. "The Human Orbitofrontal Cortex:
   Linking Rewards to Hedonic Experience." *Nature
   Reviews Neuroscience* 6 (2005). https://www.nature.
   com/articles/nrn1747

Rege, Sanil. "Obsessive-Compulsive Disorder (OCD):
   A Primer on Neurobiology, Diagnosis, and
   Treatment." 2018. https://psychscene.com/wp-content/
   uploads/2018/10/Obsessive-Compulsive-Disorder.pdf

Rolls, Edmund T. "The Functions of the Orbitofrontal Cortex." *Brain Cognition* 55 (2004). https://pubmed.ncbi.nlm.nih.gov/15134840/

Simpson, J.A., and E.S.C. Weiner, eds. *The Oxford English Dictionary*. 2nd ed. Oxford: Clarendon Press. 1989.

Chapter 14: Cutting Down Trees

Carving Pathways of Destruction

Imagine that you are standing, not in a tranquil wood, but in a forest next to a busy highway. Traffic is constantly rushing by as the highway is being expanded, and a new road is being put in.

Figure 14.1

DOI: 10.4324/9781003626725-16

Patterns of Disruption

This is a scene of repetitive stress. The term "trauma" relates to wounding, whether the injury occurs in the body, the mind, or the emotions.[1] As we saw in Chapter 7, the intersecting tree roots of the forest resemble an interconnected synaptic field. That is why, when a contiguous forest is disrupted, the overall health of the forest declines. It's like a kind of brain injury. The key is to recognize the pattern consciously so that disruption can itself be disrupted, and space can be created for peace, quiet, and recovery.

When someone has a traumatic event,
It is like a forester coming through and cutting a road,
And cutting down some of the trees.
Not all of them,
But some of them.
And then, the forest must recover.
What is underneath the forest must also recover.
The communication system must recover.

When a brain goes through a traumatic event—
Sometimes it is an experience,
Sometimes it is an accident,
Sometimes it is an illness,
Sometimes it is even a lack of proper nutrition—
It is equivalent to experiencing deforestation, to a degree.

The neural recovery process
Is like what you would see in a forest:
The forester goes through one time,

And one road goes through.
Some trees are taken,
But the forest will recover.
The next road goes in,
More trees are taken,
And it is harder to recover.
And then a big road goes through,
The land is clear cut,
And it is very hard to recover.

The more there is repetition of trauma,
The more difficult it is for the brain to regenerate,
Just like in a forest.
But, if you leave it alone,
And give it some peace,
And some space,
Some sunlight, water, nutrition, and quiet,
The natural environment will regenerate in time—
Just like the human mind.

In the watercolor painting appearing in this chapter, a hiker walks through the woods as a forester clears a path with a bulldozer. The landscape is framed by the rich brown earth and the arching limbs of the tall green trees. Within this chaotic scene, the swathe cut by the bulldozer resembles a lesion. You may recall that a similar yellow bulldozer appeared in Chapter 4. In that scene, a concrete dam was being dismantled to unblock the flow of a river. These metaphorical images show you that the same tool can be used either for disruption or for restoration, for trauma or for recovery. The same piece of mechanical equipment that tears up a forest or erects a barrier can also be used to replant a forest or to dismantle a barrier. This metaphorical imagery allows you to view the same subject from multiple perspectives at once.

Having a Foot in Multiple Worlds

While this watercolor image may be difficult to look at, it is also intriguing as a work of art. This dynamic image is both naturalistic *and* abstracted. That is, the subject matter (or iconography) of the painting is clearly recognizable, even as the forms (or formal qualities) of the image are presented in a loose, stylized manner. Neuroscientists have shown that when people engage with visual artworks, the brain prioritizes the processing of subjects that it can recognize—such as landscapes, faces, and familiar objects—and the memories associated with these subjects. Scientists believe that the reason for this prioritization relates to the evolutionary development of the human visual system. This system is associated with survival roles, including the mechanisms that enable us to quickly perceive, analyze, and understand what we are looking at, and to adapt our behaviors accordingly. When viewing works of art, researchers have not only identified the precise regions of the brain that are activated when individuals encounter recognizable subjects such as landscapes, portraits, or still lives. They have also found that people experience more pronounced brain activity when they gaze at representational images rather than at abstract ones.[2]

This is why so many of the paintings that appear in this book are purposefully *abstracted*. That is, the watercolors present familiar subjects that are easy to recognize, even as the images display the type of loosely stylized formal qualities typically found in abstract art. By adopting this hybrid stylistic approach, these *abstracted* images have a foot in multiple worlds at once. That is, because the paintings' subjects are clearly recognizable, they engage the visual and cognitive mechanisms of the brain that are associated with analysis and survival. Yet at the same time, the artworks are stylized representations of reality; they are not reality itself. Just as these abstracted images elicit the same visual and cognitive mechanisms associated with recognition and survival, they are also free of immediate survival needs. By simultaneously engaging these multiple cognitive responses, the paintings embody the concepts of multiplicity, flexibility, creativity, and transformation.

Such a dynamic perspective can be very powerful, because it can help you to detach from familiar views of a subject or situation, and allow you to see the world in a different light. Once disruptive patterns have been identified, then disruption can itself be disrupted. As a person's attention is refocused, then the forest can be reenvisioned and, ultimately, restored. Reaching such a place of transformation is not unlike giving the forest some space and water, some quiet and sunlight, so that it can regenerate in time—much like the human mind.

Exercise for Reflection and Journaling

The natural environment provides many opportunities to reflect on how human beings respond to both peaceful and stressful situations. Because I live in Houston, Texas, I have experienced many natural disasters, ranging from hurricanes and tropical storms to floods and destructive wind events. (As I have noted, life is not always a party.) Such upheavals can be traumatic because they can destroy people's homes and schools while uprooting their lives and livelihoods. Just as these events can put people under tremendous stress, I have also seen how individuals adapt and respond with both positive and negative coping behaviors.

When a storm is coming, some people become terrified and hypervigilant. They constantly monitor weather forecasts and storm tracks, and they hoard supplies. Other people make no plans whatsoever, either going into denial about the event, or optimistically just hoping for the best. None of these are balanced responses. Over time, people can learn the skills of wise planning and effective preparedness, and they can envision what resilience looks like for them. While these events are never easy, they can teach valuable lessons regarding adaptation. So many times, I have seen that people find ways to weather the storms, knowing that their world will recover and regenerate in time.

- What might it look like for you to respond to a traumatic situation in a balanced manner? What might it look like for you to respond to the same situation from a place of imbalance? How does each scenario feel? What types of behaviors emerge? Why is it important to be able to recognize these patterns when you are not actually experiencing an emergency, so that you can approach the situation from a more neutral and detached point of view?

- Are there things you can do to prepare yourself to face stressful situations? Where do you go in your mind when things become stressful? How do you create space for inner peace and quiet? Where is your sanctuary? Where are your support structures?
- Literary and visual artworks can help you to practice the qualities and related skills of multiplicity and flexibility. You can begin by creating a scene that is very precise and detailed. Then you can construct a version of the same scene that is very loose and abstracted. You can use any medium you like, whether it is painting, photography, prose, or poetry. You can also reflect on what the two scenes have in common and how they are different. You can also consider the different parts of your brain that are engaged in such activities, and why it is valuable to have multiple views of the same subject—and to have a foot in multiple worlds at once.

Notes

1 See the definition of "trauma" in the *OED*: https://www.oed.com/dictionary/trauma_n?tab=meaning_and_use&hide-all-quotations=true#17701094

2 fMRI studies show that no single or localized region of the brain is activated when viewers look at abstract art. Regarding these subjects, see Hideaki Kawabata and Semir Zeki, "The Neural Correlates of Beauty", *Journal of Neurophysiology* 91, no. 4 (April 2004): https://journals.physiology.org/doi/full/10.1152/jn.00696.2003. Regarding the specific regions of the brain associated with the processing of representational and abstract

artworks, see Oshin Vartanian and Vinod Goel, "Neuroanatomical Correlates of Aesthetic Preference for Paintings", *Neuroreport* 15, no. 5 (April 2004): https://www.researchgate.net/publication/8627374_ Neuroanatomical_correlates_of_aesthetic_preference_ of_paintings. Regarding these subjects, see also Vered Aviv, "What Does the Brain Tell Us About Abstract Art?" *Frontiers in Human Neuroscience* 8 (February 2014): https://www.frontiersin.org/articles/10.3389/ fnhum.2014.00085/full

References

Aviv, Vered. "What Does the Brain Tell Us About Abstract Art?" *Frontiers in Human Neuroscience* 8 (February 2014). https://www.frontiersin.org/articles/10.3389/ fnhum.2014.00085/full

Kawabata, Hideaki, and Semir Zeki. "The Neural Correlates of Beauty." *Journal of Neurophysiology* 91, no. 4 (April 2004). https://journals.physiology.org/doi/ full/10.1152/jn.00696.2003

Simpson, J.A., and E.S.C. Weiner, eds. *The Oxford English Dictionary*. 2nd ed. Oxford: Clarendon Press. 1989.

Vartanian, Oshin, and Vinod Goel. "Neuroanatomical Correlates of Aesthetic Preference for Paintings." *Neuroreport* 15, no. 5 (April 2004). https://www. researchgate.net/publication/8627374_Neuroanatomical_ correlates_of_aesthetic_preference_of_paintings

Chapter 15: Uprooted Ground and Tangles of Thorns

Recognizing Chaos and Despair

When a person experiences trauma and anxiety, it can feel like the ground has been ripped out from under them.

Figure 15.1

DOI: 10.4324/9781003626725-17

Broken Connections

If a person is sensitive, then they can feel the energetic connections in an environment. They can feel the sense of peace and balance—whether it is in a forest or a home— just as they can feel the sense of peace and balance within their own mind. And when the connections are broken, they can feel that, as well. Some people can break the connections and call it good. It requires a tremendous amount of denial to do so. When there is a sense of wholeness, it may feel like many notes striking one note, like many sounds making one sound.

The watercolor at the beginning of this chapter presents a suggestive metaphor for visualizing such broken connections. In this scene, a person sits wearily on the forest floor, holding their head in their hands in a gesture of despair. Even as bright green trees form a protective canopy all around them, the figure sits alone in a muddy patch of ground. Clouds of dust swirl around their head, and their feet are caught in tangles of thorny branches. All the while, a dark figure looms ominously by their side.

When a person lives in a stressful environment, they may feel trapped, scattered, and uprooted, all at the same time. When they curl up in a ball, cradle their bodies, and hide their faces in their hands, it's as though they're assuming a defensive position and attempting to shield themselves. The person may try to soothe themselves through repetitive, self-protective gestures. They may also become anxious and refuse to leave the house or get out of bed.

Seeing these patterns metaphorically can help a person to recognize them and, ultimately, to unwind them, especially if they have been wrapped up in barbed wire for weeks, months, or even years.

Sometimes the world feels closed and hard.
It may feel like the natural world has turned to concrete,
And that people are struggling
To make their way through a tangle of vines.
It's very difficult to live in such a world because,
Where is the softness?
Where is the flowing water?
How can a person live in an environment
That is so hard and closed off?

This might look like sitting in a tangle of briars,
Which is really a tangle of emotions.
This is like sitting in an old hurt,
With a pathway closed.

When a person experiences harsh conditions and rigid structures that do not resonate with them, then conflict can arise. When a person experiences trauma and anxiety, they may be calm on the outside but boiling on the inside. As the person feels the resistance rising within themselves, they may get wound up and need to be unwound. They may become anxious or obsessively controlling to manage their feelings. And then, things can get a bit scrambled.

Some people can sense anxiety and feel it, without necessarily being able to name it or put a finger on it. Some individuals can recognize that there is an energy that comes in, and that it can get out of control. It can take over their mind and emotions, making them feel uneasy or overwhelmed. These unsettled feelings can come repetitively, and they can be all-consuming. When this occurs, it is very easy to get entangled. Yet a person cannot really *do* anything until they recognize what is happening. Recognizing the pattern is key to unwinding it. As people unwind, then they can become more open to finding a new path forward.

The Art of Being in Multiple Places at Once

Both the poem and the painting appearing in this chapter provide suggestive metaphors for recognizing these disruptive patterns. This sense of recognition can allow viewers to be in multiple places at once. As we have seen, aesthetic experience engages both the brain's thinking (cognitive) and emotional (affective) centers. The creatively *abstracted* watercolors featured throughout this book activate areas of the brain associated with identification and survival, and with pleasure and reward. While different viewers will respond in different ways to the images appearing in this volume, neuroaesthetic studies have shown the specific areas of the brain that are involved with processing such complex aesthetic responses.[1] Studies have also shown that multiple responses can occur at the same time.[2] Consciously recognizing this sense of multiplicity can help a person to identify the various patterns in play so that they can begin to detach from them. This can be especially important when the responses become disruptive and scattered and there is a desire for greater unity,

Like many notes striking one note,
Like many sounds making one sound.

Exercise for Reflection and Journaling

- When life becomes difficult and stressful, how do you recognize the patterns of your responses? What words or images come to mind? What colors are they, and how do they feel? As always, record your thoughts in your journal.
- During difficult times, how do you practice self-care? Make a list of the kind actions, thoughts, and words that you extend toward yourself. Even small acts can be monumental, especially when they are performed with great tenderness. *Everyone can do this, everything matters, and everything counts.*
- How do you feel when you extend such care and kindness to yourself? If it is difficult for you to do so, spend some time reflecting on why this may be the case.

Notes

1 fMRI studies show that when people read beautiful words and when they look at beautiful images, the neural circuitry associated with pleasure and reward become activated, including "the caudate nucleus of the ventral striatum" and parts of the anterior cingulate cortex. When individuals encounter texts that they

consider to be "fearful", "disgusting", or "beautiful", then "neuronal networks systematically associated with fear and disgust (e.g. amygdala and insula), or reward and pleasure (e.g. ventral striatum, OFC)" become activated. When children read stories that elicit empathy, activation occurs in the medial and bilateral orbitofrontal cortex (OFC). Researchers have argued that the scientific data obtained from these studies supports the hypothesis that "narratives with emotional contents invite readers to be empathic with the protagonists and immerse in the text world (e.g. by engaging the affective empathy network of the brain, mainly the anterior insula and mid-cingulate cortex)" when compared to more neutral stories. For a discussion of these subjects, see Arthur M. Jacobs, "Neurocognitive Poetics: Methods and Models for Investigating the Neuronal and Cognitive-Affective Bases of Literature Reception", *Frontiers in Human Neuroscience* 9 (April 2015): https://www.frontiersin. org/articles/10.3389/fnhum.2015.00186/full

2 Regarding the multiplicity of affective response, Nancy Etcoff has noted that when people are "moved" by art, including by a sad movie, two systems of the brain that are normally kept separate can become activated simultaneously. When summarizing Etcoff's observations, Faith A. Pak and Ethan B. Reichsman have noted that

> while the person's focus is directed at a specific external stimulus (the artwork), the default mode network, which is normally active when attention is not directed at a stimulus, and consists of "mind wandering" and involves thoughts about the self,

memory, and future, is also activated. In other words, art arouses an extremely complex whole-brain response that brings into play many usually disparate aspects of the mind.

See Faith A. Pak and Ethan B. Reichsman, "Beauty and the Brain: The Emerging Field of Neuroaesthetics", *The Harvard Crimson* (November 10, 2017): https://www. thecrimson.com/article/2017/11/10/neuroaesthetics-cover/

References

Jacobs, Arthur M. "Neurocognitive Poetics: Methods and Models for Investigating the Neuronal and Cognitive-Affective Bases of Literature Reception." *Frontiers in Human Neuroscience* 9 (April 2015). https://www. frontiersin.org/articles/10.3389/fnhum.2015.00186/full

Pak, Faith A., and Ethan B. Reichsman. "Beauty and the Brain: The Emerging Field of Neuroaesthetics." *The Harvard Crimson,* November 10, 2017. https://www.thecrimson.com/article/2017/11/10/ neuroaesthetics-cover/

Chapter 16: Tying Yourself to a Reality That Makes Sense to You, and Untangling the Knots

Everyone knows the difference between a perfectly wound ball of yarn and one that is a tangled mess.

Figure 16.1

DOI: 10.4324/9781003626725-18

The Loops and Tangles of OCD

When a person experiences severe anxiety and OCD, they may lose their sense of groundedness. They may try to tie themselves to a reality that makes sense to them, to gain a sense of comfort, peace, safety, or stability. The person may perform compulsive behaviors and repetitive actions that reinforce the patterns. To be obsessed literally means to be "besieged", while a compulsion is the act of pushing and looping together. Through such repetitive "looping" patterns, a person may be seeking order yet creating chaos. They may think that they have taken a ball of yarn and gone in a straight line with it, but the patterns that they have actually created look more like some cats have batted colorful balls of yarn all around the house until everything is a tangled mess. Addressing anxiety and OCD is a bit like unwinding a skein.

OCD is an anxiety disorder that consists of obsessions, which are patterns of disturbing, unwanted thoughts or distressing images; and compulsions, which are the corresponding needs and desires to repeatedly perform actions to ease these worries or allay the intrusive thoughts.[1] The repetition of compulsive behaviors may bring some temporary relief, but these behaviors only further intensify the problem because when they are repeatedly performed, the patterns only become more deeply entrenched, both in the mind and in the brain.

The watercolors appearing in this chapter present striking visual metaphors for these states of mind and being. In the opening image, tangled skeins of yarn are shown in the same "hot" red-orange colors as the areas of heightened activity of the brain scans of people with OCD. When commenting on this condition, the psychiatrist Christopher Pittenger has noted that the brain's orbitofrontal cortex "projects to the striatum (the caudate and related structures), down to the thalamus, and back again to the cortex. It's like a positive feedback loop. And somehow, this loop is in overdrive in OCD".[2] The red and orange colors aptly convey such a sense of psychic intensity and emotional fervor, just as the two crisp, neatly wound balls of blue and green yarn evoke the relative quiet of the "cool" areas of the scans. Appearing beside the yarn are two black and white cats whose sparkling green eyes and mischievous expressions add a note of levity and charm to these otherwise heavy subjects.

Disorder and Disorders: The Psychology of Attachments

How do people get so wound up that they need to be unwound? The answers to these questions are complex, and they provide insight into the psychology of attachments— including how people absorb energy from those they are in close contact or significant relationships with. Some people who experience OCD may have had a parent who was obsessive with their own boundaries, or aggressive in their thoughts, but not particularly loving. Others may have had a parent who was extremely loving but didn't provide clear, stable, or secure boundaries. Either situation is potentially problematic. The first scenario represents power without love, while the second scenario represents love without power. Both situations are unbalanced, and both can lead to a person's feeling unsafe, and to their seeking relief and reassurance outside of themselves.

While anxiety and OCD can take many forms, the one thing that people with these conditions tend to feel is the need for relief. A person may be seeking a gentle, kind, and strong presence to help guide them, much like an ideal parent or a wise counselor. Some psychologists advocate the practice of parenting oneself—that is, becoming one's own wise parent. Sometimes this works, and sometimes it doesn't. If a person has developed a grounded adult within themselves, then they can use that aspect of their personality to be loving and to hold boundaries for the other, frightened aspect of themselves. Sometimes a person needs help from an outside source. This can be a relative, a friend, a therapist, or even a wise and loving animal.

Unwinding the Skein

A person with severe anxiety and OCD may be boiling on the inside, but they often say nothing. They may become obsessively controlling with themselves or their environment as a means to manage their emotions. They may experience recurring waves of fear or doubt and try too hard to control an outcome. Trying too hard can also be a form of fear. These patterns can create a feedback loop that can go into overdrive. Real power comes from stepping back and seeing the disordered patterns so that they can be recognized and transformed.

The word "order" is especially resonant in this context.
The root of the term is associated with weaving, with
laying "a thread on the loom" before weaving begins.
The word "disorder" is a negation of this process, as
the prefix "dis" means "not" or "none". This is why
"disorder" is the "absence or undoing of regular order or
arrangement; confusion". A disorder is also a "disturbance
of the function, and sometimes the structure, of the body,
a part or system of the body, or the mind", or "an illness
or condition that disrupts normal physical or mental
functions".[3] OCD is an anxiety disorder that can be
pictured metaphorically through these knotted loops and
tangled skeins.

In order to disentangle the pattern,
You must look at the tangle itself.
You must look at where the yarn is in a knot,
And then dig in with your fingers,
And begin to unwind and unwind.
You may think: "Oh, there's a loop here.
Let's go over, under, around, backwards, and forwards".
But first, you must notice that the entanglement is there.
And then, you can begin the exploration of unwinding it.

As you do this, there are moments when you might say,
"This is too frustrating!"
And then, you throw it all down and walk away.
A little later, you come back to it because you think,
"Oh, I know it's there.
I've just got to do it, now that I know it's there".
As you do this, you are learning how to go in and
untangle.

You are learning your own patterns,
And your own patience,
Your own tolerance,
And your own resistance.
You are learning all of it.
You are getting it all down,
So that it's all nice and straight.

After a while, you've got some beautiful yarn.
Then you can roll the skein into a nice crisp, clear ball,
And go make something nice with it.

Red, Orange, and Yellow

Neuroaesthetic studies have shown that colors can elicit strong biological and psychological responses. As Susan Magsamen and Ivy Ross have observed,

> The visual cortex, located in the occipital lobe [of the brain], controls our color perception, and colors have a biological effect on us. Red, for instance, has been shown to raise our galvanic skin response—or how much our sweat glands react—far more than colors like green or blue. . . . Colors have the capacity to change our respiration, our blood pressure, even our body temperature. Blue tends to calm our physiology and helps us to feel cooler.

Researchers have also found that yellow "promotes attention and focus".[4]

In this watercolor, the same two black and white cats now sit in a shaft of golden sunlight that streams in

Figure 16.2

through a windowpane. This is an image of warmth, peace, calm, and illumination. This image provides a suggestive counterpoint to the chaotic scene appearing at the beginning of the chapter. This metaphorical comparison can help you to visualize the difference between living *with* states of anxiety and OCD versus living *in* states of anxiety and OCD. This is like the difference between looking through the window and seeing a ray of sunlight come into the house and gently wrap around your cats versus looking directly into the hot sun at mid-day. One is soft and gentle, a reflection of warmth and kindness. The other burns your brain.

When a person is living *in* states of anxiety and OCD, they cannot fully think, feel, or know where they are. When a person is living *with* some distance and detachment from these conditions, then they have cultivated a perspective that can bring wisdom, kindness, compassion, and reflection. Once someone has experienced severe anxiety and OCD, there will never be a moment when these conditions are not part of their life story. The wisdom of the experience will always be remembered. Yet the person will no longer be living in a tangled mass of disordered skeins. They will be free to pick up the yarn and go make something nice with it.

Exercise for Reflection and Journaling

- In Part Two of this book, disordered emotional patterns appear metaphorically as tangles of vines and knotted skeins of yarn. What metaphors come to mind for you as you picture these disruptive, repetitive patterns? What colors are they, and how do they make you feel?
- Whether or not anxiety or OCD are issues in your own life or in the life of someone you know, it is very powerful to learn about these subjects and to recognize the various forms that they can take. This is also where journaling can be helpful. Journaling provides a protected space to practice the skills of close observation, clear description, and a sense of multiplicity that can lead to detachment. This can potentially allow for greater mastery and self-control.

Notes

1 For a general discussion of "Obsessive-Compulsive and Related Disorders", see: https://med.stanford.edu/ocd/about/understanding.html

2 Christopher Pittenger, "What Does an OCD Brain Look Like?" *Yale School of Medicine* (October 10, 2014): https://medicine.yale.edu/news-article/what-does-an-ocd-brain-look-like/

3 According to the *OED*, the etymology of the word "order" references the classical Latin *ōrdin, ōrdō* as being "perhaps cognate with *ōrdīrī* to lay the warp before weaving, to initiate (an enterprise)", and that *ōrdō* originally denoted "a thread on the loom". See the entries on "order" and "disorder" in the *OED*: https://www.oed.com/dictionary/order_n?tab=etymology#33283106 and https://www.oed.com/dictionary/disorder_n?tab=meaning_and_use#6602841

4 Susan Magsamen and Ivy Ross, *Your Brain on Art: How the Arts Transform Us* (New York: Random House, 2023), 40–41.

References

Magsamen, Susan, and Ivy Ross. *Your Brain on Art: How the Arts Transform Us*. New York: Random House. 2023.

Pittenger, Christopher. "What Does an OCD Brain Look Like?" *Yale School of Medicine*. October

10, 2014. https://medicine.yale.edu/news-article/
what-does-an-ocd-brain-look-like/

Simpson, J.A., and E.S.C. Weiner, eds. *The Oxford English Dictionary*. 2nd ed. Oxford: Clarendon Press. 1989.

Chapter 17: Old Haunts and Sour Fruits

Visualizing Anxiety and OCD

When a person experiences severe anxiety and OCD, it may feel like they are haunted by a menacing presence that hovers over them and follows them around.

A Fiendish Opponent

The psychiatrist Jeffrey M. Schwartz has aptly characterized OCD as a "devilish disorder" and as a "deceptive opponent" that is "fiendishly clever".[1] In several of the illustrations appearing in this book, OCD is presented metaphorically as a "haunt"—that is, as a large, dark, twisted figure with a gaping mouth and dendritic limbs that resemble the grasping hands of a stunted tree. Sometimes this presence looms ominously in the foreground, while sour fruits dangle from its withered limbs.

DOI: 10.4324/9781003626725-19

Figure 17.1

The Haunt

According to the *Oxford English Dictionary*, a haunt is at once a spectral presence, a repeated habit, and a place that is frequently visited. This term refers to "unseen or immaterial visitants", including not only ghosts but "diseases, memories, cares, feelings, [or] thoughts". Haunts are also unwelcome visitors that "come up or present themselves as recurrent influences or impressions, especially as causes of distraction or trouble". As a verb, to "haunt" something means to practice it frequently, including to do or to use something as a habit. A haunt is also the location where the patterns occur. Thus, an old haunt is "a place of frequent resort or usual abode", including "the usual feeding-place of deer, game, fowls, etc.".[2]

When a person experiences severe anxiety or OCD, they may think that they are afraid of one thing—such as a specific disease, or form of contamination, or type of risk. Yet what they may actually be afraid of is being consumed by a destructive, out-of-control energy that has no kindness or care—like a haunt.[3] The important point to remember is that, ultimately, OCD only wants to be fed, and its hunger will never be satisfied. Engaging in repetitive behaviors will not keep a person safe, healthy, or comfortable. Just as this condition does not have a person's best interests at heart, the more that the patterns are fed, the stronger they will become. A person's real power lies in the choices they make. Sometimes this means choosing *not* to do something, such as engaging in repetitive behaviors that only perpetuate the pattern. Refusal can be a very powerful tool once a pattern is clearly recognized.

Building the Light of Consciousness

When a person experiences challenging situations, one of the best things that they can do is to identify the energies in play. Nothing can be done until the condition is identified and acknowledged. Then different choices can be made, and behaviors can be changed.

A person with severe anxiety or OCD
May be sitting in the darkness of unconsciousness.
Yet when dark thoughts arise in a person's mind,
Then they get to choose what to do with them—
How they respond and react.

Patterns are built up over time,
Based on what a person chooses to do.
Does the person take on the darkness?
Do they integrate it into their own being?
Do they think, "Oh, I like that feeling!
I'm going to absorb it".
Or do they think, "I don't like that feeling!
I'm going to reject it".
Do they choose to carry the darkness,
Or do they choose not to carry it?
Do they choose to feed it,
Or do they choose not to feed it?
The power lies with the one who chooses.

Both people and places can feel like they are haunted by old patterns.
A sensitive person can feel the emotional energy of an environment.

When you step into certain places,
You can feel the heaviness, the weight,
And even the terror that exists there.
And then, you can step into other places and feel the
lightness.
You may think, "What a lovely, wonderful place to be!"

Something similar can happen in a person's mind.
With consciousness, a person can have a sense of,
"Oh, I'm doing this now!"
"Oh, I'm doing that now!"
Then real change can happen.
A person can disentangle themselves from fear.
It all comes from building the light of consciousness.

Exerting the Need for Control

People with severe anxiety and OCD will often seek to
control difficult or uncertain situations, including those over
which they have little to no control. At its root, the term
"control" signifies a counter-roll (*contre* + *role*). Historically,
this term refers to a duplicate copy of a roll, scroll, or other
official document that was kept for the purposes of record
keeping or for management through surveillance.[4] The term
"control" literally signifies a back-and-forth process of cross-
checking—of continually reading one scroll or roll against
another. When performed with care and balance, this practice
can help to manage a complex situation responsibly. When
not in balance, control can become associated with excess,
domination, bullying, and endless critique. People can
become overpowered and haunted by the need for control.

Figure 17.2

Jeffrey M. Schwartz has observed that the repeated thoughts and urges associated with OCD have a "ferocious intensity" that reflects the overactive nature of this neural feedback loop.[5] One intriguing way to visualize these subjects is to imagine two ancient Roman officials wearing togas and holding scrolls, while endlessly cross-checking one another's accounts, and speaking to each other with bullying rigor and "ferocious intensity".[6] As the two officials continually judge and criticize each other, they repeat the same behaviors over and over until the patterns are deeply entrenched. *Does that sound like a healthy relationship to you?*

Jeering Illusions

When a person engages in such endless cross-checking, they may feel dominated and dispirited. Giving in to such negative thoughts and repetitive behaviors may offer the promise of temporary safety and comfort, but this is only an illusion. The word "illusion" relates to jeering and mocking, especially to playing badly with someone. An illusion is a deception, an act of creating false appearances in the body or in the mind. An illusion is also a phantom or apparition; it is a mental state of giving reality to something that is inherently unreal.[7] The haunting presence of OCD speaks in a language of illusions, making false promises in a jeering voice that demands control but only offers the sour fruits of temporary relief.

Picking New Fruit

Some people do not like ambiguity. The mind wants to go with what it knows, with what it has repeated, and with what has brought some relief in the past. When a person repeats a compulsive behavior, then they may think that they are picking the fruits of relief, but ultimately, that is only an illusion.

Dealing with severe anxiety and OCD is a gradual process. The key is to recognize how the patterns appear, and how they repeat themselves. Then it is possible to recognize the triggers and to formulate alternative responses. Through care and consciousness, a person can see how the energies are cultivated and fed, and how the patterns are built up over time. Questioning one's own behavior is a key step. A person can consciously stop and ask themself: "Do I really want to do this? I know that if I do this, I will not be satisfied. So, what in this moment will bring me true relief?"

At some point, a person must decide for themselves that the fruits are sour—that they taste like biting into an unripe mango—and that there is nothing new to learn or to taste there. The person must refuse to give in to the obsessive thought. They must decide that there is no need to look obsessively at the same thing over and over again, or to endlessly repeat the same act and expect a different outcome. Once a person recognizes this, then they can take their eyes off of the haunt and approach life differently.

As they do this, they are building trust. They are trusting themselves not to repeat old patterns. They are trusting themselves not to revisit old haunts. They are trusting themselves to ask different questions and to get different answers. They are trusting themselves to pick fruit off of new trees.

Exercise for Reflection and Journaling

Once disruptive patterns are identified and recognized, then different choices can be made. The images in this chapter provide striking visual metaphors for seeing and describing states of mind and body that can be subtle and thus difficult to see. With these themes in mind, you can ask yourself:

- What triggers my repetitive patterns?
- How do I feel when I repeat these patterns? Is this what I really want?
- If I were to create a metaphorical portrait of anxiety or OCD, what would it look like? How would the pattern appear? What clothes would it wear? What colors would it be? What would its voice sound like?
- If engaging in this obsessive behavior was like eating food, what would it taste like? Would it be fresh and sweet, or would it be stale and bitter? What would it smell like?
- If you are tempted to indulge in a repetitive behavior, in your mind's eye, you can imagine a haunt offering you sour fruit, like an unripe mango. Then imagine yourself taking a bite of the fruit. It may satisfy your craving for a moment, but that moment is fleeting, and you're likely to feel a bit sick afterward. *When OCD arises, the key is to recognize what is happening, to refuse to perpetuate the pattern, and to do something different, knowing that you are making a different choice.*
- As you work with this metaphorical imagery, carefully record your thoughts and feelings in your journal so that you have a clear record of your patterns and your progress.

Notes

1 See Jeffrey M. Schwartz's vivid description of OCD in *Brain Lock* (New York: HarperCollins, 2016),

xxxviii–xl. In a related audio book (Audible, 2016), Schwartz characterizes OCD as a curse that carries a plague of symptoms, and he personifies this condition as a tyrant, a bully, and an aggressor that intimidates the naïve and the uninitiated.

2 See the entries on "haunt" in the *OED*: https://www. oed.com/dictionary/haunt_v?tab=meaning_and_ use#2131159 and https://www.oed.com/dictionary/ haunt_n?tab=meaning_and_use#2130687

3 The writer Eckhart Tolle characterizes such energy as a "pain-body". Tolle describes a pain body as an unconscious component of the human ego, "a deeply negative energy field" that lives inside a person, craves their attention, and engages them in the "energies of suffering". The keynotes of this emotional pattern include irrationally heightened negative feelings such as fear, anger, and sadness. Tolle advocates that when the pain-body arises, the best responses are awareness, recognition, and compassion. See Tolle's lecture on "How the Pain-Body Affects Relationships": https:// www.youtube.com/watch?v=5jSpDZVM1WE

4 See the entries on "control" in the *OED*: https://www.oed.com/dictionary/control_n?ta b=etymology#8252087 and https://www.oed. com/dictionary/control_n?tab=meaning_and_ use#8252087 and https://www.oed.com/dictionary/ control_v?tab=meaning_and_use#8253842

5 Schwartz, *Brain Lock*, xlvi.

6 This illustration is loosely based on the *Mosaic of Virgil*, a marble mosaic dating from the early third century that was found on the archaeological site of the

ancient North African city Hadrumetum. The mosaic shows the Latin poet Virgil holding a scroll containing a fragment of his epic poem the *Aenid*. In the mosaic, he is flanked by Clio and Melpomene, the muses of history and tragedy, respectively. The mosaic is currently housed in the National Bardo Museum in Tunis: http://www.bardomuseum.tn/index.php?option=com_conte nt&view=article&id=78%3Avirgile&catid=43%3Alat ine-romaine-&Itemid=74&lang=en

7 The etymology of "illusion" descends from the Latin *il* + *lūdĕre*: to play. See the entries on "illusion" in the *OED*: https://www.oed.com/dictionary/illusion_n?tab=meaning_ and_use#968463 and https://www.oed.com/dictionary/ill usion_n?tab=etymology#968463

References

Schwartz, Jeffrey M. *Brain Lock*. New York: HarperCollins. 2016.

Simpson, J.A., and E.S.C. Weiner, eds. *The Oxford English Dictionary*. 2nd ed. Oxford: Clarendon Press. 1989.

Tolle, Eckhart. "How the Pain-Body Affects Relationships". https://www.youtube.com/watch?v=5jSpDZVM1WE

Chapter 18: Like Birds with Open Wings

Holding On by Letting Go

Imagine that you are standing in a clearing in a forest. As you look up, you see a flock of birds swirling overhead. You then think to yourself, "This is grace itself".

Unfettered Freedom

This is the kind of experience that a person might have, not while they're walking next to a busy highway, but when they're standing in a thousand acres of pristine wilderness. This type of environment can create a sense of peace and calm, and an inner silence that quiets the mind. As a person takes their eyes off of the chaos, they can look at the world differently. And then, real transformation can begin.

The watercolor at the beginning of this chapter depicts such a moment of clarity and illumination. As a person looks up, they see something new. Above the tall pine trees, a flock of doves with outstretched wings swirls gracefully in the golden sunlight. Grace can be seen, not only in the delicate movements of the birds' wings, but in the energy that inspires the person to turn their head and look up in the first place.

DOI: 10.4324/9781003626725-20

Figure 18.1

Seeing Something New

Every person has had such a moment of epiphany—a moment of pure bliss when the mind stops, time seems to stand still, and a new sense of presence emerges. This could be during a beautiful sunset, or on a snowy morning, or on a holiday. It doesn't matter where and when the experience occurred. The important thing is that *everyone* has had such a moment of transcendence. These experiences can feel joyful, powerful, and protective. They can inspire us to raise our vision, and they can ignite our desire for change. Sometimes people's eyes and minds become so riveted by fear that they need to ask for help to look up and see something new. This can be as simple as looking up at the sky and saying, "Please help me. I want to see something new".

Living with OCD is, in part, a journey of faith. Having faith means having the capacity to tolerate a certain degree of uncertainty, and to accept the unknown. This can entail having faith in oneself, in life, and in a connection to something greater than oneself. A person with anxiety and OCD may be seeking to connect with something more powerful and joyful than the anxious or controlling part of their own mind. Some people find such peace and strength in nature. For some, a tree can be an angel, and the sky can be heaven. For others, a connection with a special animal can serve as a connection to life itself. A cat or a dog or a bird or a horse can be your transcendent—a protective presence that creates space to be vulnerable, and that allows your heart to go into softness. For others, transcendence can look like the sacred figures of established religious traditions. And for others still, transcendence can look like images of pure love, such as gazing into the eyes of a cherished person, or a newborn child.

A Sliver of Light Was Still Getting Through

In my work with people at the end of life, all of these images of transcendence arise on a regular basis, and sometimes several images coalesce within a single narrative. Whatever form they take, the stories are always powerful, and they are always beautiful. Sometimes people at the end of life will also tell me about the challenges that they have experienced, including their struggles with anxiety and OCD.[1] I am now going to present a composite narrative that engages these themes from multiple perspectives at once. The artwork blends the voices of three different people, all of whom told me similar stories. This is a combined narrative of letting go of old patterns, and of finding a new path forward.

One day, I met a woman who told me about how her fears had interfered with her daily living and her cherished relationships with her family. Yet a few years prior, the woman experienced a powerful epiphany, and this imagery formed the basis of her narrative. Her artwork is called *A Sliver of Light Was Still Getting Through*. As she recalled:

> *When I was growing up, my family was very poor.*
> *We had very little, and we struggled.*
> *I had to work hard from the time I was young.*

*I always wanted to make sure that there would always
be enough,
And I knew that I wanted something better for my family.*

*So, I started saving up and accumulating things.
Things would pile up,
And then I'd have to keep checking on them,
To make sure they were still there,
And that everything was still okay.
It could be bank balances,
Or it could be important papers,
Or it could be valuable things in the house.
Sometimes I couldn't even sit down
And get through an entire dinner with my family
Without having to get up and check.*

*Sometimes I'd even get up in the middle of the night,
To make sure everything was still there,
And that it was all still okay.
I'd write myself little notes of reassurance,
But that didn't work.
I was still really afraid, inside.
Sometimes I couldn't fall back asleep again,
And I'd be tired all the next day.*

*I had reached a point where I was exhausted.
I wasn't owning the stuff.
The stuff was owning me.
These things were all dragging me down,
Because the fear was dragging me down.*

*I saw this clearly one night,
When we were all sitting down to dinner together.*

My family was just sitting at the table,
And I noticed a cabinet in the corner.
Some boxes were piled up so high
That they were nearly blocking out the dining room window.
But, not quite.
I could still see a little bit of light coming through.
A sliver of light was still getting through, at the top.

And then I realized:
It's just stuff.
It's no big deal.
It's not the soul.
I could see what matters,
And what doesn't.
That was an inspiration.
It came by just looking up at the window,
And just looking up at the sky.

To Find Relief Is to Be Uplifted

People who suffer from severe anxiety and OCD are often looking for such relief. To experience relief is to be uplifted and restored. Sometimes just looking up can provide a sense of relief, as it did for this woman. Relief is a state where pain and distress are lessened so that the mind and the body can be put at ease. Literally, to be relieved means to be lifted up, to rise again, and to be restored to an upright position (*re + lever*).[2] Relief also relates to bringing support "for a besieged place; to free from siege or attack". As we saw in Chapter 16, to be obsessed literally means to be "besieged". Looking up and asking for help can be both uplifting and inspiring. As a person looks up, they are looking for something strong and bright, both inside and outside of themselves.

Like Angels With Open Hands

In this watercolor, the landscape has transformed into a visionary scene. As a person stands in the middle of a forest, the bright blue sky becomes a site of freedom and expansion. As sunlight bounces off the birds' feathers, little bits of gold seem to be swirling in the air. An avalanche of grace seems to be falling from the sky.

As the person looks up, they notice a cloud formation that resembles an angel with outstretched wings and open

Figure 18.2

hands. The figure on the ground below spreads out their own arms and hands in a reciprocal gesture of exchange. Old patterns are given away and burdens are released into the sky—to the birds with open wings, and to the angel with open hands. This transformative scene depicts the art of holding on by letting go.

Exercise for Reflection and Journaling

- When things become very difficult, there are a few practical steps you can take: First, consciously recognize that you are feeling anxious or having fearful thoughts. Then, acknowledge that you do not want to feel this way. Refuse to let the thoughts take hold of you. Close your eyes, breathe gently, and ask for help. Then step back from your own anxious thoughts, as if you were watching yourself take a step backwards. Quiet your mind, look upward, and allow yourself to receive the help that you asked for. When the moment has passed, express gratitude for the assistance you received. Then go and do something different.
- Many images of presence and transcendence appear throughout this chapter, including in the shifting, subtle forms of clouds, birds, and angels. Because this imagery is so fluid and dynamic, it is the imagery of transformation. The important thing is to consider how such images of transformation and transcendence appear to *you*. How do you personally experience a connection to something greater than yourself?
- Where does true relief—that magical combination of comfort and uplift—lie for you? What do joy and

transcendence look like for you? How do you picture yourself looking up? What words do you use, and how do they make you feel?

- How do you visualize the very beautiful paradox of holding on by letting go? Within your own life, what do you want to hold onto, and what do you want to let go of?

- Let's consider a practical example: If, like the woman in the story, you find that accumulation, overcrowding, and holding on too tightly are issues for you, you can always use words and images to practice the art of holding on by letting go. If including too much information or excessive detail is an issue, try writing two versions of the same story, or creating two versions of the same image. Choose a subject that intrigues you and work with whatever medium you feel drawn to. In the first artwork, create an extremely detailed scene or narrative. Then, create a second version of exactly the same image or story, but one that is far more spare and economical. Use your strong will to be selective in what you keep and what you let go of. Even if it is hard for you to resist adding additional details, just know that you already have one detailed image or story, and that you are now consciously creating something new. You are leaving more space for openness, breathing room, and flexibility.

- As you work with these concepts, can you imagine observing the story or situation from a more elevated and detached perspective? Can you see this as part of a larger learning experience? Can you imagine saying to yourself, "I have learned what I need to learn from this experience, and I am grateful to have had it. I am now ready to let this go and move on". If it is not yet the right time for you to do so, just keep these thoughts in mind for the future. If it is the right time, then consider erasing some of the lines of your drawing or editing some of the sentences of your story. Do this with great consciousness and clarity of intention. How much do you really need to hold onto? See yourself unwinding the pattern as you erase the lines or cut the words.

- Even if this experiment doesn't work the first time, be proud of yourself for being open to it, and be proud of yourself for trying. Then, try again. All the while, know that you are consciously working with the very beautiful and challenging paradox of holding on by letting go.

Notes

1 The poetic case study presented here resonates with, yet is stylistically different from, the memoirs of people suffering from anxiety and OCD. A well-known example within this literary genre is Daniel B. Smith's best-selling book *Monkey Mind: A Memoir of Anxiety* (New York: Simon & Schuster, 2012). While recounting his personal experiences of trauma and anxiety, Smith describes the Buddhist concept of the "monkey mind", which relates to the pervasive anxiety associated with "excesses of thought and emotion". As Smith vividly puts it,

A person in the throes of monkey mind suffers from a consciousness whose constituent parts will not stop bouncing from skull-side to skull-side, which keep flipping and jumping and flinging feces at the walls and swinging from loose neurons like howlers from vines. Buddhist practices are designed explicitly to collar these monkeys of the mind and bring them down to earth—to pacify them.

(p. 27)

For a literary survey of the writings of people with mental illness, see Nathan Carlin, *Pathographies of Mental Illness* (New York: Cambridge University Press, 2022). The mental health conditions covered in this volume include "depression, bipolar disorder, schizophrenia, substance use disorders, borderline personality disorder, conduct disorder, antisocial personality disorder, autism spectrum disorder, and eating disorders". (p. 1). In this volume, Carlin adopts a comparative approach that pairs the individual narratives with related discussions from the *Diagnostic and Statistical Manual of Mental Disorders* (*DSM*).

2 See the entries on "relief" in the *OED*: https://www.oed.com/dictionary/relief_n2?tab=etymology#25981796 and https://www.oed.com/dictionary/relief_n2?tab=meaning_and_use#25981796

References

Carlin, Nathan. *Pathographies of Mental Illness.* New York: Cambridge University Press. 2022.

Simpson, J.A., and E.S.C. Weiner, eds. *The Oxford English Dictionary*. 2nd ed. Oxford: Clarendon Press. 1989.

Smith, Daniel B. *Monkey Mind: A Memoir of Anxiety.* New York: Simon & Schuster. 2012.

Chapter 19: Fly-fishing in the Trout Stream

Letting Yourself Off the Hook

It takes a lot of energy to stay present when it is difficult to do so.

Figure 19.1

DOI: 10.4324/9781003626725-21

Fishing Around in One's Mind

In this watercolor, a person stands in a beautiful forest, fly-fishing, while a haunt looms menacingly in the foreground. In this scene, the person is not just standing in a river, but in the flowing stream of their own thoughts. While the water appears to be blue, it is actually composed of all colors. The stream holds everything because it is the flow of life itself.

If a person experiences severe anxiety or OCD, then they may be fishing around in their mind for distressing thoughts or disturbing memories. As they do this, they can always hook a negative thought, reel it in, and feed the haunt. Yet with consciousness, patience, and practice, they can make different choices. They can choose to stand in the stream and stop fishing. They can let the distressing thoughts off the hook and watch them flow downstream.

In this image, the person's red-orange fishing gear calls to mind the "hot" areas of the brain scans of people with OCD. As we have seen, when a person is experiencing this condition, the brain's orbitofrontal cortex appears to be caught in an overactive feedback loop. In this painting, the fisherman concentrates all their attention on a single patch of the stream, thereby placing their energetic focus in one location. Metaphorically, it's as if they are reinforcing a particular neural pathway, which creates a positive feedback loop that can be either constructive or destructive. The person can either reenforce established OCD patterns, or they can consciously shift their focus and change their behavior.

As pain is transmuted through practice, old patterns can unwind. This is not easy, but it is worth it. It is another example of the transformative art of holding on by letting go.

The Art of Staying Present

Shadows hate the light of consciousness,
Because they cannot hold themselves together in this light.
Meeting your shadow in the light of consciousness
May mean that you just have to sit there,
And stay with the uncomfortable thoughts and feelings that arise,
Whether they evoke worry, fear, sadness, anxiety, or anything else.

You just have to stay present and sit with these emotions.
You just have to say: "I'm here with you.
I'm not rejecting you.
I'm not trying to get out of you.
I accept you, and I feel you".
When you meet these energies in the light of consciousness,
You begin to transmute them.

This practice requires patience, focus, energy, care, and mindfulness.
You cannot multitask.
You cannot look at your phone.
You cannot do forty-five other things in that moment.
You simply have to sit there and wait it out,
As the thoughts and feelings flow by.

This practice will show you exactly where your attachments lie,
And where your stories are most deeply anchored
Within the patterns of your own identity.

When you release the stories
That are anchoring the anxiety and the OCD,
*Then you are letting **yourself** off the hook.*
You are watching your thoughts flow downstream
Into the beautiful running water.

There's a Trick to All This

While you're doing this practice, you have to be careful not to allow your rational mind to start analyzing the thoughts and feelings that arise. This analytical approach won't work because it is only a distraction. It's a way of getting out of having to *feel* the uncomfortable feelings, while simultaneously amplifying them. Analysis can always come later. As painful thoughts and emotions arise, you just have to sit there in the light of consciousness, witnessing the patterns, feeling the feelings, waiting them out, and letting the images and feelings flow by.

Memory Is Like a Woodblock Carving

Why do we go fishing around, in our minds and in our memories? Why is it so difficult to let go of old patterns that we truly don't want and that don't serve us? Patterns of thought and behavior can easily become woven into our system. While we may remember our experiences as being a certain way, our memories can be changeable. We continually rewrite history, even in our own minds. What lasts are the deepest impressions.

Imagine that a printmaker is creating a woodblock carving. As the artist cuts the initial design onto the smooth block of wood, the more deeply the pattern is carved, the greater the impression it will make. More ink will flow into the empty spaces where the block has been cut most deeply. When paper is run over the ink-filled parts of the woodblock, the most deeply carved areas will hold the greatest amount of ink. These areas will create the darkest, clearest, strongest, and most long-lasting impressions. The deeper the pattern is cut and the more deeply the impression is made, the longer it will last—whether it is in a woodblock print, or in a neural pathway.

Yet, what about the fainter areas surrounding the deeply carved impression? When it comes to our memories, our minds constantly refill the spaces around the primary subject. As years go by, we refill a lot. We tend not to think about the fainter areas of the impression as much as we do about the parts that feel indelible. As time passes, these seemingly indelible structures can become like a grounding place. The memories can be deeply woven into a person's identity, including their definitions of who they are and how they relate to the world. If they were to let these patterns go, they may feel a bit shaky. It could feel like an indelible aspect of the person was lightening and fading, and possibly even disappearing—and that can make a person feel nervous. Then they may realize,

Not only do I have to redefine myself. I also have to admit that I have defined myself by what it feels like to be in these experiences. But then if I let them go, I'm not quite sure who I am, in relationship to myself, to my past, and to the world around me. It all feels a bit shaky.

This is why healing is a gradual process. There is only so much that a person can do at a time. Energetic patterns are built up over time, and a river cannot be transmuted in a day. A person's energy and identity can continue to stabilize as they release old patterns and reprogram the mind, the brain, and the body. When a person begins to let go of old patterns, there may be a period of feeling uncertain. Different sensitives can be reawakened when we drop the armor of our old identities and our old stories. When we are carrying around less armor, we feel lighter, and perhaps a bit more vulnerable and sensitive. We also feel more fluid and graceful. We are standing in the flow of life. We are practicing the art of holding on by letting go.

Exercise for Reflection and Journaling

When fearful thoughts or disturbing images arise, you can always look closely at the watercolor painting in this chapter and practice the fly-fishing meditation. If it is easier for you to listen than to read, then read the meditation aloud and record yourself as you practice this exercise:

Picture yourself standing in a beautiful stream,
Wearing red-orange fishing gear.
You are watching your own thoughts and feelings flow by.

As you stand there,
Are you fishing around in your mind for negative
thoughts?
Are you hooking them,
And reeling them in,
And feeding the haunts of anxiety and OCD?

If you find yourself doing this,
Picture yourself doing something different.
See yourself standing in the stream,
Just watching the water flow by.
Meet your thoughts and feelings with great care and
kindness.
Just feel them and watch them float past.

While this practice may be uncomfortable,
And of course, you want out,
You don't get out.
You just stand there in the stream, and you wait it out.
As you stay present with your thoughts and feelings,
You are transmuting them.
As you let these thoughts off the hook,
*You are letting **yourself** off the hook.*
You are watching the energies flow downstream,
Into the beautiful running water.

Like any other skill, this takes time, energy, patience, and
practice. Because you can only do so much at a time, it is
important to keep a record of your progress. Make special
note of how long you are able to stand in the stream of
your own thoughts and allow them to flow by before
reeling in a distressing thought or performing a repetitive

action. Gradually try to increase the amount of time you stand there, letting the thoughts and emotions flow by. Remember that, rather than repeating what you already know, you are learning something new. Do not judge yourself or be unkind to yourself. You are practicing the art of graceful detachment. You are transforming the landscape of your own mind and brain.

Chapter 20: Going Through the Forest with a Garbage Bag

Clearing Old Ground

It takes a lot of courage to make new choices and to clear old ground.

Figure 20.1

DOI: 10.4324/9781003626725-22

A Road That Anyone Would Love to Walk on

People with anxiety and OCD often tell themselves the same stories over and over again, as if on repeat. Yet the repetition of the familiar narratives only tends to generate more anxiety. Throughout this section of *Neuroaesthetics and the Art of Transformation*, the looping patterns of unwanted thoughts and repetitive behaviors have been depicted metaphorically as debris—as knotted skeins of yarn, as barbed wire, and as thorny tangles of vines and brambles. The repetition of the old stories creates entrenched neural pathways that are like littered roads that have been deeply dug into the forest floor. Yet when a person releases the stories and clears old ground, it is like they are walking through the forest with a trash bag, taking out the garbage of the mind and the emotions.

In the watercolor appearing in this chapter, a figure walks through the forest toting two enormous, overflowing black trash bags. As the person gathers the trash and clears the ground, the path in front of them gets smoother, easier, and gentler. This is a landscape of transformation. There is a new sense of hope and renewal. Previously, the pathways were much busier. Now, some of the unneeded pathways have grown in. Little groves of saplings and little patches of grasses and wildflowers grow in the no longer used pathways. Everything is calmer and clearer, because the person is not allowing doubt and fear to lead them this way and that, and to spin them in all different directions. This is now a road that anyone would love to walk on.

Clearing the Landscape of the Mind

When a person has been rolling around in severe anxiety and OCD, a tremendous amount of doubt gets built into the system. This energy scatters the mind, ungrounding the person and disrupting their connection to themselves.

Unwinding from old patterns means looking at yourself differently,
Especially if you have been wrapped in barbed wire
For weeks, months, or even years.
As you unwrap yourself from the intensity of these wounding thoughts,
It is important to be patient and open
To finding a new path forward.
You may need to recognize your patterns in the moment,
And say to yourself, "Oh self, I see that this is where we are today.
I accept how hard it is for you.
We are building the momentum of change".

You cannot reprogram the mind by doing the same things over and over.
Clearing old patterns and releasing illusions means that
There needs to be time for quieting the mind,
For unplugging what no longer needs to be plugged in,
And for cultivating peace, contentment, ease, and grace.
When a person cleans up their thoughts and clears old ground,
Extra resources can then be given to what they want to grow,
To what they want to cultivate.

Sometimes when a person cleans up old ground,
They revisit old haunts.
Old patterns may be retriggered as the debris is being
cleared away.
Yet now the person notices that these thoughts no longer
have such a strong grip,
Or such powerful traction in their life.
They trust their own mind not to go off in all directions,
Down rabbit holes and into lairs that do not serve them.

As a person clears the shadows of old attachments,
The light gets so bright that they can actually see their
own emotions.
Then they can ask themselves,
"Oh, what was that shadow moving around?"
As the light shines brighter and brighter on the shadow,
The shadow diminishes,
And the person builds their light of consciousness.

Exercise for Reflection and Journaling

- As you practice clearing old ground and cleaning up the garbage of the mind and the emotions, imagine that you are walking through a forest with an enormous black trash bag. See the distressing thoughts and feelings as litter. Watch your hand grab a chunk of this tangled, mucky debris and throw it into the garbage bag. When the bag is full, imagine yourself throwing the heavy bag into a giant dumpster. Feel your hand release the garbage bag, feel your shoulder relax, and hear the bag go "thunk" as it hits the bottom of the dumpster.

- How would you describe the debris in your garbage bag? What color is it? What does it look like? What does it smell like?
- How do you feel as you let go of the trash bag and you hear the resounding "thunk"? What emotions arise? As always, record your thoughts and feelings in your journal. Practice this exercise as often as you need to.
- How is this exercise part of the transformative art of holding on by letting go?

Chapter 21: Taking a Good Bath and Starting Fresh

Practicing Self-Care

The processes of moving stuck energies and clearing old ground can feel a bit like running clear water through muddy water.

Figure 21.1

DOI: 10.4324/9781003626725-23

After a while, the water flows easily. Because this flow is both purifying and transformative, it can reach places where nothing else can reach.

Changing one's thoughts and behaviors is hard work.
When a person has finished their work for the day,
They may find that they are dirty from head to foot.
It's like they are covered in muck and grime.
Then it is time to return to the mansion of one's thoughts
For some nurturing and self-care.

In the mansion, a nice hot bubble bath is waiting.
The person gets into the water.
It cleanses them as the water soaks in.
As the water goes deep into the muscles,
The person relaxes and releases.
As they lie there in the tub,
They let go of all the things
That made them muck and grime in the first place.

By the side of the tub,
A soft pink towel is draped over a comfortable chair.
Nearby, a new set of clothes is all laid out.
The clothes are made of fine cloth
Beautifully woven with golden threads.
Everything fits perfectly,
And everything is made with love.

Exercise for Reflection and Journaling

- How do you practice acts of cleansing and self-care?
- Imagine that you are dirty from head to toe. You prepare a nice hot bubble bath for yourself. In your mind's eye,

see yourself get into the tub and wash off all the muck and grime. Allow the water to sink deeply into your muscles. Feel yourself becoming completely relaxed. After a while, you see that you are clean because you have washed off everything that made you grimy in the first place. How do you feel now?

- When you're finished, see yourself stepping out of the tub and drying yourself very gently with the softest, warmest pink towel imaginable. Then see yourself donning a new set of clothes, which have been made just for you. Return to this meditation any time you want to feel cleansed, nurtured, and refreshed.

- If you were to design your own magical bathroom, what would it look like? How would the room be laid out? What style of furniture would it hold? In the watercolor, the bubble bath has a pale violet tint. What colors flow from the taps of your bathtub? Remember, this is a *magical* bathroom. It is a sanctuary. In this restorative space, you can always clean off and start fresh, because the atmosphere is purifying and transformative.

- How is this meditation part of the transformational art of holding on by letting go?

- Now that you have reached the end of Part Two of this book, revisit the question of how reading this book is an act of self-care. Go back and reread the journal entry that you made following Chapter 13, where you noted your hopes and goals for this section. What have you learned? Has your perspective changed as you have explored these important subjects? What adjustments have you made, if any, and why? How do these changes make you feel?

Part III: Deer Trails Through the Woods

Finding a New Path Forward

Chapter 22: When Compost Becomes New Soil

Neuroplasticity

Throughout our lives, we learn and we grow. From the struggle and the change come the richness, and there is new life.[1]

Figure 22.1

DOI: 10.4324/9781003626725-25

Neuroplasticity and the Art of Transformation

All around us, life is constantly changing, requiring us to adapt. The term "neuroplasticity" refers to the transformative nature of the brain. This term describes the nervous system's ability to "form and reorganize connections and pathways, as during development and learning, or following injury".[2] In the watercolor appearing at the beginning of this chapter, a gardener plants some brightly colored blossoms in soil that has been cleared of debris and carefully cultivated. Both the figure and the forest all around them appear in soft shades of cool blue and green, while the flowers emerge as vibrant pops of red, orange, and yellow. As we saw in Chapter 13, these warm shades evoke the "hot"—or active—areas of the brain scans of people with OCD, while the cool tones indicate the places where less energy is being consumed. As the gardener focuses on their landscaping activities, the garden becomes a space of renewal, promise, and transformation.

Upgrading Bad Wiring

When a person's thoughts and behaviors are not serving them well, a great deal of energy is flowing into circuitry that is not working for them. You can think of this as a kind of bad wiring. When old patterns dissolve and become obsolete, then the energy that was being used to keep the patterns going is no longer being consumed. This energy then becomes available for many other uses, including for healing the mind and cultivating the plasticity of the brain.

Neuroplasticity refers to the processes of structured growth and the forming of new connections, both through learning and through healing. When a person quiets their mind and recognizes and releases unwanted thoughts and behaviors, then they can reset themselves internally. The person can choose to go and do something creative and rewarding. As rewiring occurs, new pathways are made. Depending on the person's character, they can choose to focus their energies on gardening or painting, singing or dancing, playing sports or music.

Sometimes people work very hard to release old patterns.
Eventually, people reach a place where the mind
Has built up enough momentum for remapping.
New information can come in,
And it can rewire some of the ways that the person
interacts with the world.
You can think of this as a kind of recoding—
An upgrade in the electrical system of the body.

In life, everyone faces challenges,
And they hit milestones where they get upgraded.
When a person gets upgraded, a new pathway is made,
And what runs through the structure of the brain is
transformed.

Increased awareness can be one type of upgrade.
As a person becomes much more aware of their own
story and motivations,
They are able to rewire their patterns more quickly.
They may also become much more aware of other
people's motivations,

And their alarm bells may go off more frequently
As they place more trust in their own knowing.

Plasticity, in the Arts and in the Brain

In the fine arts, the term "plasticity" is associated with pliable materials that can be easily molded and sculpted into a variety of creative forms. In biology, plasticity refers to the "adaptability of (part of) an organism to changes in its environment; specifically, the ability to alter the neural connections of the brain as a result of experience, in the process of learning, etc.".[3] In both contexts, to be plastic is to be flexible, creative, and adaptable. The mind and the brain are inherently dynamic and transformative, and new neuronal connections can form throughout a person's life.[4] The synapses—or the junctions between nerve cells—can be strengthened or weakened over time as their activity increases or decreases. Just as the brain is capable of such remarkable plasticity, it has a great capacity to learn, to heal, and to create.

As a person works through their thoughts and emotions, they can always express whatever needs to be expressed in an artful manner. Even dark thoughts and painful emotions can be expressed with great imagination. All the tools of the creative arts—rhythm, sound, pattern, color, form, and expression—offer rich possibilities for such expression and transformation. This is why the arts hold so much power to shape the mind and to help a person move through life with grace and fluidity.

We all know what it is like to speak with someone who is
stuck.
There is no plasticity there.
And we all know what it is like
To speak with someone who has plasticity.
There is movement and flexibility.

Children's brains have so much plasticity.
There is so much capacity for expression—
For play, dance, joy, and emotion.
Expression is constantly moving through them.
Things don't get stuck.

Depending on our personality,
As we age, the brain can get very stuck.
And then, the energy moving through the brain
Is split in so many different directions.
There's so little energy left available
For healing, for transmutation, or for an epiphany.

Plasticity is the energy of movement and change.
As you move through time, you can learn
How to become more malleable and graceful.
You can become more like a dancer who keeps on
dancing,
No matter what song is playing.

Even as the music is always changing,
The dancer flows with the rhythm.
They see themselves move through something in life,
And they say to themselves,

"Oh, I understand this enough now to know
That this is moving through me,
And I am moving through it.
No matter what song is playing,
I say yes to the music.
I am dancing with the flow of life".

In this watercolor, a dancer is shown surrounded by loose fields of abstract color. You can think of these delicate tonal fields as metaphors for the various experiences and emotions that arise in life. Just as the dancer's body is flexible and graceful, it is also extremely strong and skillful. The dancer appears like a beautiful sculpture. No matter what arises—no matter what music is playing—the dancer can adjust, adapt, and continue. She says yes to the music, and she dances with the flow of life.

Figure 22.2

Exercise for Reflection and Journaling

- Neuroplasticity refers to the processes of structured growth and the forming of new connections through the reframing of one's focused attention combined with their conscious practice. In this chapter, neuroplasticity is depicted metaphorically through the activities of gardening and dancing. What metaphors come to mind for you? What new things do you want to develop or cultivate in your own life?

- Are there difficult experiences or painful emotions that you can imagine expressing artfully and with great intention? How might you use rhythm, pattern, sound, color, and form as tools for working through complicated emotions, so that you can express whatever needs to be expressed in an artful manner?

- You can reflect on the amazing power of your own neuroplasticity as you imagine dancing with the flow of life. How do you envision yourself dancing, even as the music keeps changing? What is uniquely beautiful about this image, and what makes the dance your own? As always, record your thoughts, images, and reflections in your journal.

- If you were to create your own neuroaesthetic artwork, how would you imagine a landscape whose structures and patterns resonate with those of the mind and the brain? If you were to visualize the landscape of your own mind, what would it look like, and why? Where would the light be falling? What features of the landscape are uniquely your own, and what do they share with all of humanity?

Notes

1 In my book *The Colors of Life*, I explore these concepts in relation to the color black. See Marcia Brennan, *The Colors of Life: Exploring Life Experience Through Color and Emotion* (New York: Routledge, 2025), 107–108.
2 See the definition of "neuroplasticity" in the *OED*: https://www.oed.com/dictionary/neuroplasticity_n?tab=meaning_and_use#1211991520
3 See the entry on "plasticity" in the *OED*: https://www.oed.com/dictionary/plasticity_n?tab=meaning_and_use#30043950
4 Neurotransmitters are associated with both neuroplasticity and synaptic plasticity. They include acetylcholine, which "facilitate[es] neuroplasticity across the cortex", and astrocytes, or "star-shaped glial cells", which "are known to release a variety of different neurotransmitters into the synapse to help foster synaptic plasticity, when required". Regarding these subjects, see Kayt Sukel, "Neurotransmission: Neurotransmitters": https://dana.org/app/uploads/2023/09/fact-sheet-neurotransmission-neurotransmitters-baw-2020-1.pdf. See also Kendra Cherry, "Neurons and Their Role in the Nervous System", *Verywellmind*, October 2023: https://www.verywellmind.com/what-is-a-neuron-2794890

References

Brennan, Marcia. *The Colors of Life: Exploring Life Experience Through Color and Emotion.* New York: Routledge. 2025.

Cherry, Kendra. "Neurons and Their Role in the Nervous System." *Verywellmind*. https://www.verywellmind.com/what-is-a-neuron-2794890

Simpson, J.A., and E.S.C. Weiner, eds. *The Oxford English Dictionary*. 2nd ed. Oxford: Clarendon Press. 1989.

Sukel, Kayt. "Neurotransmission: Neurotransmitters". https://dana.org/app/uploads/2023/09/fact-sheet-neurotransmission-neurotransmitters-baw-2020-1.pdf

Chapter 23: I Have Visions Most People Don't Have

Reenvisioning the Relations Between Beauty and Trauma

Sometimes beauty and trauma can appear—not as opposites—but as distinctive aspects of a single experience.

One day I met a man whose outlook on life was very positive, even as he faced the very end of his life. This man had spent his entire professional career as a land steward who cultivated both pine and hardwood trees through sustainable foresting practices. The man loved taking care of the trees and shaping the landscape. Contemplating the long-term possibilities of the forest taught him how to see the world in a different light, an approach that was helping him greatly. As he said:

I Have Visions Most People Don't Have

Being a land steward means shaping the land.
I love changing the scope of the landscape,
And making it better.

DOI: 10.4324/9781003626725-26

Figure 23.1

You have to take care of the trees.
I have visions most people don't have.

Most people look at a piece of land,
And they can't see what it will look like a few months
from now.
Most people can't see this vision.
But I can.

This experience has been a blessing.
Most people don't look up until they get on their backs.
I've always thought of that as I've taken care of things.

Life is wonderful.
I couldn't have asked for better.
I have visions most people don't have.

Just as the man approached life with great thoughtfulness and care, his story simultaneously encompasses multiple points of view. When reading his words, it is possible to imagine standing on level ground, looking out across the expanse of the forest, surveying the trees. Yet given the circumstances of the story's production, it is equally possible to imagine the man lying flat on his back in his hospital bed, seeing the forest in his mind's eye as he looked up at the ceiling. And just as this story contains both a naturalistic and a visionary perspective, it is also possible to imagine viewing the forest panoramically, as if looking down from a bird's eye point of view.

If you practice holding these multiple perspectives simultaneously, you can see how different points of view can crystalize into a single image or narrative. Much like the synaptic field of the interwoven tree roots that thread through a forest floor—imagery that we examined in Chapter 7—the man saw an interconnected field of possibilities underpinning a living landscape. This complex perspective allowed him to be in multiple places at once, and to integrate experiences of beauty and trauma. This gave the man a vision of life that most people don't have. And now that you've read the story, you have this vision, as well.

It's All Part of the Same Story

The watercolor painting appearing in this chapter depicts a tall tree with a missing limb and some missing bark. Even as the tree is showing its age a bit, it is still majestic, it is still firmly connected to the forest, and it is still beautiful. Its roots sink deep into the earth, while its limbs reach up to the sky. Both the tree's roots and its limbs are like antennae. They are like fingers or feelers that touch the world, both above and below. The tree is surrounded by filtered sunlight, and a deer stands poised to drink from the stream of water that flows so gently by its side.

You would never walk up to a tree with a missing limb,
Or with some missing bark, and say:
"You are no longer pretty to me.
You are no longer beautiful".
Instead, you would say, "Oh, this is your story.
Wonderful! This is all part of your beauty.
Your age is showing a bit.

Therefore, I will think of you as wise.
You have been here a long time.
I see that you have gained awareness and perspective.
This is all part of your story,
And part of your wisdom".

In the poem and in the watercolor, seemingly opposite qualities are present at the same time. These qualities include beauty and trauma, immediacy and timelessness, the natural and the visionary. The artworks literally sit in multiple places at once. Recognizing this complexity can help you to expand your perspective. Just as the arts can help you to recognize that many different subjects can all be part of the same story, the artworks can inspire an expansive sense of peace, calm, resilience, and renewal.

Following the Trails of People's Thoughts

"I Have Visions Most People Don't Have" is an end-of-life story that centers on the themes of cultivation, care, gratitude, and the capacity to hold multiple perspectives at once. When I visit with people at the end of life, I can often see the deep grooves of their thought processes. These are the pathways that people won't get off of, or that they won't let go of. These are the patterns that are the most deeply entrenched, both in the mind and in the brain. Sometimes these pathways are painful, and sometimes they are beautiful.

As the functionality of the body diminishes,
And the brain gets quieter at the end of life,

A person is left with the most ingrained patterns of the mind.
If kindness is deeply grooved,
It will be there.
If trust and surrender are deeply grooved,
They will be there.
If courage and vulnerability are deeply grooved,
They will be there.
If cynicism, doubt, anger, and suspicion are deeply grooved,
Then they will dominate the person's experience.
It all becomes incredibly evident at the end stages of life.
This is why it is important to notice your own pathways of thought—
How they look, and how they feel—
Because this is a beautiful motivation for life itself.

Seeing Life from Multiple Perspectives

Another way to practice the art of holding multiple perspectives at once is to look at color and at black and white versions of exactly the same image. Which one do you prefer? Both images hold intriguing possibilities. The black and white drawing leaves more room for a person to fill in their own color. The image leaves more space for the depths of the viewer's imagination. Yet sometimes in life, the opposite is true. Sometimes the depths and beauty of the color image excite a person's mind beyond what they could imagine on their own. At other times, the color version is shallower than what a person could imagine for themselves.

Figure 23.2

Figure 23.3

The same is also true with words. Sometimes writers use very simple language, assuming that readers will use their imagination to fill in the details as they read. Sometimes the reader does, and sometimes they don't. Sometimes it feels like flavor has been added to the words so that a person reads with heightened emotion. Then the reader may experience a stronger reaction, or they may take the story further in their own mind.

As we have seen, neuroaesthetic studies have shown that processing complex meanings in both prose and poetry can promote nuanced and dynamic modes of thinking. Researchers have also found that reading literary texts can contribute to a person's ability to create new meanings, to cultivate a more flexible perspective, and to formulate alternative conceptual frameworks.[1] As you experiment with these possibilities—as you consciously observe your own reactions to different artworks, or to color and black and white versions of the same image—it is as though you have a window into your own mind. You are experimenting with being in multiple places at once.

The Transformative Power of Color

Another intriguing way to engage these subjects is to approach the black and white image as part of an adult coloring book. As discussed in Part Two, different colors produce different effects, both in the mind and in the brain. Hot colors tend to warm and excite us, while cool tones tend to create a sense of peace and calm. Scientists have shown that coloring can also be used as an effective technique to reduce stress and anxiety. In one study, researchers compared the psychological and psychophysiological benefits of coloring and drawing by measuring people's heart rates, breathing rates, and skin conductance. Scientists found that both coloring and drawing can reduce anxiety and create enjoyment in measurable ways.[2]

Another study found that observing harmonious combinations of colors can produce a pleasurable response in the brain, while disharmonious color combinations can elicit negative reactions. Through fMRI technology, scientists pinpointed the "neural correlates of color harmony and disharmony"—or the places in the brain where emotional responses to color combinations are registered. As the researchers concluded: "Results showed

Figure 23.4

that the left medial orbitofrontal cortex (mOFC), and left amygdala [and right posterior insula] were activated when participants observed harmonious and disharmonious stimuli, respectively".[3] As we have seen, the amygdala is the part of the brain associated with emotional responses to stimuli, and the orbitofrontal cortex helps to assess and process sensory information and to integrate this knowledge into learning and behavioral patterns. Just as these neuroaesthetic insights can help you to see the same subject in different ways, they can help you to know yourself better, to calm your mind, and to expand your own thinking. Not only is this very powerful, but it can give you a vision of life that most people don't have.

Exercise for Reflection and Journaling

Throughout this book, subjects are approached in multiple ways at once—through the arts and the sciences, through prose and poetry, through words and images, and sometimes, through black and white and color versions of the same image. As you engage with these themes, you are actively working through multiple analytical and creative modalities. You are also practicing the art of being in multiple places at once.

- In your journal, record your reflections on, and your responses to, the color and the black and white images of the tree. Why is each one powerful, and what are the limitations of each medium? Which version are you drawn to and why? How does your imagination fill in portions of the black and white image? Is the color image more intense than you might have been able to imagine for yourself? What do you notice when you consciously go back and forth between the two modes?

- Make copies of the large black and white image of the tree and approach this drawing as part of an adult coloring book. Observe whether the act of coloring helps you to cultivate a sense of peace and calm. Note your responses in your journal.

- Experiment with selectively filling in sections of the black and white image with harmonious color combinations, and then, with disharmonious ones. In your eye and in your mind, which tones blend harmoniously and which color combinations clash? How do these combinations relate to your own preferences, to your own sense of taste, and to your own state of mind? Why is it powerful to know that your personal emotional responses register not only in your eyes and in your mind, but also in the amygdala and the left medial orbitofrontal cortex of your brain? How do these concepts help you to be in multiple places at once?

Notes

1 In one study, fMRI techniques were used to assess neural mechanisms as people both derived and reappraised meaning while reading prose and poetry. The researchers found that "enhanced literary awareness is related to increased flexibility of internal models of meaning, enhanced interoceptive awareness of change, and an enhanced capacity to reason about events". They also speculated that such brain activity may be related to "tolerance of uncertainty". These qualities can be

important for people with mental health difficulties, for whom

meaning derivation tends to be biased by dysfunctional and rigid beliefs. The encouragement to consider alternative and nuanced meanings through active reading of texts may generalize to encourage more adaptive, less rigid and biased meaning derivation in everyday life; thus facilitating mental health and wellbeing.

See Noreen O'Sullivan et al., " 'Shall I Compare Thee': The Neural Basis of Literary Awareness, and Its Benefits to Cognition", *Cortex* 73 (December 2015): 144–157: https://www.sciencedirect.com/science/article/pii/S0010945215003081

2 See Nicole Turturro and Jennifer E. Drake, "Does Coloring Reduce Anxiety? Comparing the Psychological and Psychophysiological Benefits of Coloring Versus Drawing", *Empirical Studies of the Arts* 40, no. 1 (May 2020): https://journals.sagepub.com/doi/10.1177/0276237420923290. This research was prompted by the popularity of adult coloring books. In 2015, *Adult Coloring Book: Stress Relieving Patterns* (Bend, OR: Blue Star Press) became a *New York Times* bestseller. Regarding these subjects, see also Susan Magsamen and Ivy Ross, *Your Brain on Art: How the Arts Transform Us* (New York: Random House, 2023), 40–43.

3 Takashi Ikeda et al., "Color Harmony Represented by Activity in the Medial Orbitofrontal Cortex and Amygdala", *Frontiers in Human Neuroscience* 9 (July 2015): 1–7: https://www.frontiersin.org/articles/10.3389/fnhum.2015.00382/full

References

Blue Star Coloring. *Adult Coloring Book: Stress Relieving Patterns.* Bend, OR: Blue Star Press. 2015.

Ikeda, Takashi, Daisuke Matsuyoshi, Nobukatsu Sawamoto, Hidenao Fukuyama, and Naoyuki Osaka. "Color Harmony Represented by Activity in the Medial Orbitofrontal Cortex and Amygdala." *Frontiers in Human Neuroscience* 9 (July 2015): 1–7. https://www.frontiersin.org/articles/10.3389/fnhum.2015.00382/full

Magsamen, Susan, and Ivy Ross. *Your Brain on Art: How the Arts Transform Us.* New York: Random House. 2023.

O'Sullivan, Noreen, Philip Davis, Josie Billington, Victorina Gonzalez-Diaz, and Rhiannon Corcoran. "'Shall I Compare Thee': The Neural Basis of Literary Awareness, and its Benefits to Cognition." *Cortex* 73 (December 2015): 144–157: https://www.sciencedirect.com/science/article/pii/S0010945215003081

Turturro, Nicole, and Jennifer E. Drake. "Does Coloring Reduce Anxiety? Comparing the Psychological and Psychophysiological Benefits of Coloring Versus Drawing." *Empirical Studies of the Arts* 40, no. 1 (May 2020). https://journals.sagepub.com/doi/10.1177/0276237420923290

Chapter 24: Webs of Connection and Protection

Spider Lilies and Arachnoid Mater

Both in our lives and in our brains, flowers can appear as symbols of strength, protection, and connection.

Figure 24.1

DOI: 10.4324/9781003626725-27

Last and First Things

One day, I met a lovely woman whose husband lay in the Medical Intensive Care Unit, facing the very end of his life. I invited the woman to tell me something wonderful about her husband, and we created a tribute to him. This couple lived in a lake house on forest land in East Texas. This landscape has its own unique flora. As the woman told me about the various trees and plants that grew on their property, her thoughts became focused on one particular flower—the orange-red spider lily. When I asked her what made this plant so special, the woman's description of the flower became the final words of her tribute to her husband, and a symbol of their life together:

Spider Lilies: The First Flowers of the Season

My husband loved to garden,
And the first flower of the season—
He'd always bring it to me.
It's an orange-red spider lily.
I'd wait for the first blooms to appear each fall.
It is so hot and miserable in July and August
That most everything else just gives up.
But not this lily.

The spider lily is really the last flower of the season,
But I call it the first.
In the fall, after everything else has died,
This is the first flower
That comes back.

The watercolor painting appearing at the beginning of this chapter displays rich clusters of orange-red blossoms surrounded by soft green grasses and vibrant accents of bright blue. Just as this scene is dynamic, its subjects are heart-opening. As you read the story, you can feel the man's loving attention as he hands his wife the lily, and you can feel their hearts open to one another. This gesture feels like a rebirth after a time of retreat, after a period of turning inward—both at the end of the summer, and at the end of life. As you feel the strength and renewal of their connection, you may feel your own heart open, as well.

Shortly after our visit, the woman sent me a photo of orange-red spider lilies blooming prolifically on their property. The spider lily, which is also known as the resurrection lily, is associated with the arrival of autumn.[1] The woman's story shows that even at the very end of

Figure 24.2

life, we can still see flashes of red, and we can still feel associations of passion, vitality, strength, endurance, hope, renewal, and love. These qualities are also evident in the perseverance of the perennial flower bulbs. In this story, the spider lily appears not only as a symbol of the couple's love and their life together, but also as a reflection of the paradoxical nature of ends and beginnings. Just as the spider lily is both the last *and* the first blossom of the season, it represents a beauty that survives when all else falls away.

Protective Coverings

The spider lily is named for the spindly structures of its blossoms, which resemble spider legs. Just as the term "arachnid" refers to spiders, in our bodies, the arachnoid mater serves as one of the three protective membranes, or meninges, that cover the brain and the spinal cord.[2] The thick, outermost membrane is called the dura mater; it sits under the skull bone and helps to hold the brain in place. The soft, thin, innermost layer is called the pia mater; this membrane covers the brain and the spinal cord with a protective cushion of cerebrospinal fluid.[3] Between the two layers lies the arachnoid mater, whose delicate fibers resemble spider webs. Cerebrospinal fluid flows under the arachnoid mater in a region of the brain called the subarachnoid space. Just as the arachnoid mater serves as "a network for communication between the systemic venous [or vein] system and the cerebrospinal fluid" of the brain and the spinal cord, this membrane creates a vital

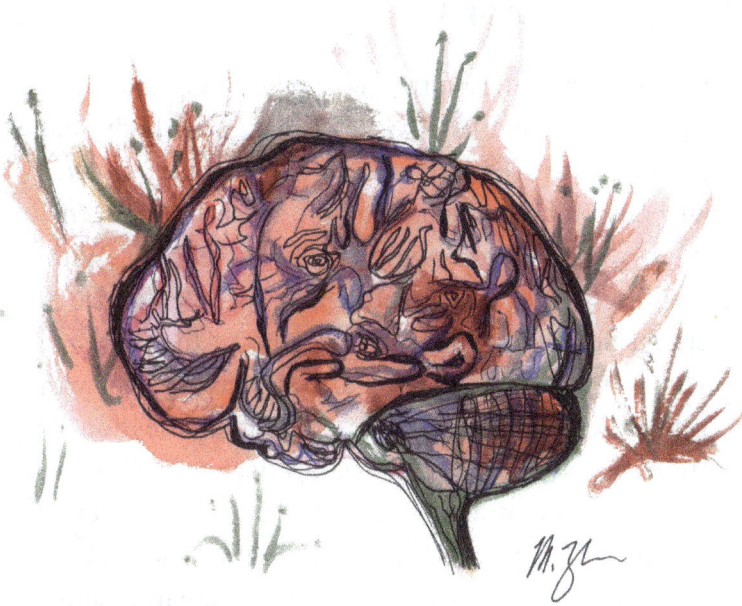

Figure 24.3

web of fluid connection and a protective covering within the body.[4]

This watercolor presents an imaginative view of how the arachnoid mater sits atop the pia mater, while covering the vulnerable surfaces of the brain's gray and white matter. In this image, patterns of stylized webbing appear to be overlaid atop a human brain. The outer design resonates with the forms of spider lilies, while the stalky green brainstem evokes the leaflike sepals that enclose the flower petals. This painting can help you to visualize how intricate webs of connection and protection are woven throughout our bodies, our lives, and the natural world.

Changing Fiber Into Form

While the membranes surrounding the brain and the spinal cord provide protective coverings *inside* our body, the clothing that we wear covers and protects the *outside* of our body. When we contemplate these interwoven domains, we encounter many layers of meaning. Within the creation stories of the Indigenous peoples of the American Southwest, the sacred figure of the Spider Woman is associated with the art of weaving and with the gifts of wisdom, education, and communication. In traditional Navajo practices, "before weavers sit down at the loom, they often rub their hands in spiderwebs to absorb the wisdom and skill of Spider Woman".[5] A great and rich history is associated with these creation stories. The narratives describe how the spider first taught human beings to weave fabric, and how to form words from symbols. People recognized that networks of lines could be used to create the symbols that form writing. By watching the spider make webs, humans learned how to make knots, and how to change fiber into both form and language.

Such images evoke the ways in which interwoven structures form living networks of protection and connection, both in our bodies and in our lives. Just as the things that we love and value the most can have a protective feeling for us, such webs of support can protect and sustain us through all phases of life.

When a child sees a flower in the springtime,
They often cannot help but bring it to their mother.

*The flower could be a violet, a daisy, a dandelion, or a
spider lily.
It is an act of pure love from the heart of the child.
Love is the ultimate protection,
The ultimate connection,
And the ultimate communication.*

*Arachnoid mater is also protective.
It connects different aspects of the brain and the body,
While communicating in subtle ways.
Throughout our lives, the webbing of the brain reforms
and regenerates.*[6]
*When everything is moving smoothly and purely,
Unobstructed and undiminished,
It flows like the love of a child.*

*As adults, we remember the completely generous acts of the
child,
The times that we said, "I thought of you.
I bring this to you as a symbol of the love I feel for you,
Which I pour out to you at this moment".
Throughout our lives,
We aspire to the purity of that childlike love,
And to the strength of the connections
That protect us, both inside and out.*

Exercise for Reflection and Journaling

- Living webs of connection, protection, and
  communication are woven throughout our inner and
  outer worlds. Look carefully at the image of the spider
  lily, then look closely at a spider web. What do these

structures have in common? After you identify their similarities, call up an image of the arachnoid mater online and notice the similarities that you see within the body, as well. How do these explorations reveal resonant networks of connection and communication, both in the body and in the natural world?

- Videos of Navajo weavers are readily available online. Watch some of the videos and notice how the artists expertly turn fiber into form. As they weave, ask yourself: How are the artists creating webs of communication and connection on the material, visual, and symbolic levels, all at once? How is their activity like that of a spider weaving its web, and how is it different?

- In the illustration accompanying Chapter 16, a tangled mass of yarn appears as a metaphor for the looping patterns of OCD. As discussed in that chapter, individuals with OCD often attempt to tie themselves to a reality that makes sense to them. As they do so, they can create great disorder in their life. How are these tangled strands of yarn fundamentally different from the intricate, orderly patterns that you observe in the spider webs, the spider lilies, and the arachnoid mater? How are the tangled skeins also very different from the yarn that the master weavers use as they turn fiber into form?

Notes

1 The scientific name of the spider lily is *lycoris radiata*. Regarding this flower, see the University of Florida's entry on the "Hurricane Lily" (2022): https://gardeningsolutions.ifas.ufl.edu/plants/ornamentals/

hurricane-lily.html. For traditional practitioners of Buddhism, the flower is associated with the ceremony held at the tombs of ancestors, as red spider lilies are planted on and around grave sites. See Atsutaro Ito, *Great Japanese Plant Illustrated Volume 1* (Dainippon Botanical Illustrated Publishing Company, 1911–12), frames 44–51: https://dl.ndl.go.jp/pid/1908225/1/44

2 See the entries on "meninges" found on the Mayo Clinic website and in the *OED*: https://www.mayoclinic. org/diseases-conditions/meningioma/multimedia/ meninges/img-20008665#:~:text=Three%20layers%20 of%20membranes%20known,is%20called%20the%20 dura%20mater and https://www.oed.com/dictionary/ meninx_n?tab=meaning_and_use#37256951

3 Victor Kekere and Khalid Alsayouri, "Anatomy, Head and Neck, Dura Mater", *StatPearls*, 2023: https://www. ncbi.nlm.nih.gov/books/NBK545301/#:~:text=The%20 meningeal%20layer%20of%20the%20dura%20mater%20 creates%20several%20dural,of%20dura%20in%20 the%20brain

4 Jack Y. Ghannam and Khalid A. Al Kharazi, "Neuroanatomy: Cranial Meninges", *StatPearls*, July 2023: https://www.ncbi.nlm.nih.gov/books/ NBK539882/#:~:text=Arachnoid%20Mater,-The%20 arachnoid%20sits&text=Its%20structure%20 consists%20of%20a,fibers%20within%20their%20 intercellular%20space

5 See the entry on "Spider Woman" in *UXL Encyclopaedia of World Mythology*, vol. 5 (Detroit: Gale, 2009), 963–965. Regarding these subjects, Leleua Loupe notes: "The intricate patterns of the web that Spider Woman weaves teaches followers to look for the

patterns in the world, the power of connection, and that all beings are creations and therefore relatives, making survival tied to respect for all life". See Leleua Loupe, "Spider Woman", in *Women in American History: A Social, Political, and Cultural Encyclopaedia and Document Collection*, vol. 1 (Detroit: Gale, 2017), 66–67. Within Greek mythology, the goddess Athena is associated with the arts and crafts of spinning and weaving.

6 Regarding these processes, see Ilaria Decimo et al., "Meninges: From Protective Membrane to Stem Cell Niche", *American Journal of Stem Cells* 1, no. 2 (2012): 92–105: https://www.ncbi.nlm.nih.gov/pmc/articles/PMC3636743/

References

Decimo, Ilaria, Guido Fumagalli, Valeria Berton, Mauro Krampera, and Francesco Bifari. "Meninges: From Protective Membrane to Stem Cell Niche." *American Journal of Stem Cells* 1, no. 2 (2012): 92–105. https://www.ncbi.nlm.nih.gov/pmc/articles/PMC3636743/

Ghannam, Jack Y., and Khalid A. Al Kharazi. "Neuroanatomy: Cranial Meninges." *StatPearls*, July 2023. https://www.ncbi.nlm.nih.gov/books/NBK539882/#:~:text=Arachnoid%20Mater,-The%20arachnoid%20sits&text=Its%20structure%20consists%20of%20a,fibers%20within%20their%20intercellular%20space.

Ito, Atsutaro. *Great Japanese Plant Illustrated Volume 1.* Dainippon Botanical Illustrated Publishing

Company, 1911–12, frames 44–51. https://dl.ndl.go.jp/pid/1908225/1/44

Kekere, Victor, and Khalid Alsayouri. "Anatomy, Head and Neck, Dura Mater." *StatPearls*, 2023. https://www.ncbi.nlm.nih.gov/books/NBK545301/#:~:text=The%20meningeal%20layer%20of%20the%20dura%20mater%20creates%20several%20dural,of%20dura%20in%20the%20brain.

Loupe, Leleua. "Spider Woman." In *Women in American History: A Social, Political, and Cultural Encyclopaedia and Document Collection*, edited by Peg A. Lamphier and Rosanne Welch, vol. 1, 66–67. Detroit: Gale. 2017.

Simpson, J.A., and E.S.C. Weiner, eds. *The Oxford English Dictionary*. 2nd ed. Oxford: Clarendon Press. 1989.

"Spider Woman." In *UXL Encyclopaedia of World Mythology*, edited by Condino Meggin and Rebecca Parks, vol. 5, 963–965. Detroit: Gale. 2009.

Chapter 25: Networks and Lattices

Rose Arbors and Neuronal Arborization

Since antiquity, roses have served as symbols of beauty, grace, wisdom, love, power, and self-protection.

Figure 25.1

DOI: 10.4324/9781003626725-28

Structures of Integration

Just as roses have great natural beauty, they shed light on the concept of integration. Rosebushes grow in dark soil, and their stems are covered in sharp thorns. These flowers are naturally very well-protected. Once you are pricked by a thorn, you approach this plant with great care and gentleness from that point onward.

In the watercolor painting appearing at the beginning of this chapter, a rose tree growing on a trellised arbor is juxtaposed with a diagram of neuronal arborization. The branching stems of the rose bush resonate with the structural patterns of the neuron. Just as "arbor" is the Latin word for tree, a dendrite is a branching tree-like form. In the brain, dendritic arborization is the process through which neurons form branching patterns to create new synapses, or new connections between nerve cells.[1] Scientists have observed that as dendrites branch outward from a cell body, "they usually form tree-like arborizations around the neuron", thereby creating a formation known as a "dendritic tree".[2] The specific forms that the patterns take help to determine how neural circuits are formed, and what types of inputs a neuron can receive.[3] Not only do different neurons have different branching patterns, but the overall shape of the arbor "is one of the crucial factors determining how signals coming from individual synapses are integrated"[4]—or how different messages are received and processed in the body.

The structures of arborization are extremely important for our health and well-being, as well as for our growth and learning. As researchers have shown, neuronal arborizations are "essential for the connectivity between neurons that underlies normal brain functions",[5] particularly those involving networking and communication processing, since "receiving inputs, processing information, and learning and memory formation all depend on the complexity of the dendritic arbor".[6] In turn, many neurodevelopmental disorders—including epilepsy, schizophrenia, autism spectrum disorders, Alzheimer's disease, and Parkinson's disease—are associated with disrupted arborizations and synapse formations.[7] Both in the brain and in the rosebush, arborization represents a vital structure of integration, connection, and communication.

Integration and Transformation

In the opening watercolor, roses appear in various stages of budding, growth, and decay. Some of the flowers are blossoming, while others are fading, and their petals are dropping to the ground.

> *When you look at a rose, you see harmony.*
> *You see beauty.*
> *You see evolution.*
> *You see magnificence.*
> *You never question the rose.*
> *Even as the blossom is opening,*
> *And then turning,*
> *And then beginning to decay and fall—*
> *There is still beauty in the cycle of it all.*

You don't question that.
Yet somehow, we don't always see ourselves that way,
Especially when we are in disharmony.
We don't see our own cycles of blossoming and
expansion,
Or our own growth and beauty.
We might only see what we're doing wrong,
Or how we're not doing well enough.
Too often we don't see our own turning of the seasons,
Or our own stages of growth,
Or our own transformation.

When a person can see the bigger picture in life—when
they show compassion, understanding, kindness, and love

Figure 25.2

for themselves and for others—they can feel themselves expanding. Because these changes relate to the inner parts of a person's character, these intrinsic qualities don't appear on the outer surfaces of the body. Yet it is possible to imagine how a person's subtle inner qualities can be visualized externally.

In this delicate watercolor, a figure stands in a garden amidst latticed pink roses. The figure appears, not as a detailed portrait, but as an abstracted presence who blends with the flowers around her. This is a scene of creative transformation. It is as if the figure's vibrant *inner* qualities appear on the *outer* surfaces of her body as loose fields of abstract color. Watercolor readily lends itself to such creative explorations and to such fluid possibilities. Just as the flexibility of the medium is all part of its beauty, watercolor can help you to envision new possibilities for making otherwise invisible presences visible.

As a person detaches from their familiar stories, they generate space for something new to emerge—something softer, wiser, gentler, kinder, and more integrated. These transformations can be visualized in the mind's eye. Look at an image of a flowering rosebush, and then soften your gaze until the forms blur and the flowers become colorful abstractions. Imagine that these subtle fields of color are overlaid like a luminous, transparent layer over your own face. As you work with this metaphor, you can imagine yourself becoming, not the rose, but the energy *of* the rose.

Exercise for Reflection and Journaling

- Look carefully at the structures of a rosebush, including its stems, branches, buds, leaves, petals, and rose hips. How is the overall form of the rosebush an example of arborization and integration? How does the rosebush appear like a miniature tree whose overall forms resonate with the structures of the brain and the nervous system? Why is it intriguing to engage in such creative analogical thinking? How can this skill help you to expand your vision, and to see the world in a new light?
- Once again, look carefully at the structures of a rosebush, including its stems, branches, buds, leaves, petals, and rose hips. Rose hips are the small round areas of the rose that remain after the petals have fallen. Rose hips are the fruits of a rose, and they contain the seeds that grow into new rosebushes. After looking carefully at the individual structures of the plant, take a step back and look at the rosebush holistically. How is every part of the plant beautiful, including the parts that are not normally considered to be so? No matter what stage any part of the plant is in, it reflects a crucial phase of life itself. How might you apply these insights to your own life, learning, and integration processes?
- In your mind, you can practice becoming, not the rose, but the subtle energy *of* the rose. Recall a time when you handled a difficult situation with strength, grace, and compassion. Remember that these qualities are also associated with roses, historically. Take a photograph of your face and then add soft, transparent layers of watercolor wash over your features. Choose colors

that hold special significance for you. As you apply the delicate washes like veils of color, imagine that you are watching your own *inner* qualities becoming expressed on the *outer* surface of your body. How does this exercise help you to see yourself differently, and to recognize the beauty of integration, both inside and out?

Notes

1 Regarding the structures of neuronal arborization, see Malgorzata Urbanska, Magdalena Blazejczyk, and Jacek Jaworski, "Molecular Basis of Dendritic Arborization", *ACTA Neurobiologiae Experimentalis* 68 (2008): 264–288: https://ane.pl/index.php/ane/article/view/1695/1695

2 On this subject, see Krishnagopal Dharani, *The Biology of Thought: A Neuronal Mechanism in the Generation of Thought* (Cambridge, MA: Academic Press, 2014), 115.

3 Regarding these subjects, see the work of the Development Group Research at the University of California San Francisco: https://janlab.ucsf.edu/development-group-research#:~:text=Dendrite%20arborization%20patterns%20are%20critical,mental%20disorders%20such%20as%20autism

4 Urbanska et al., "Molecular Basis of Dendritic Arborization": https://ane.pl/index.php/ane/article/view/1695/16955

5 Ane Goikolea-Vives and Helen B. Stolp, "Connecting the Neurobiology of Developmental Brain Injury: Neuronal Arborisation as a Regulator of Dysfunction and Potential Therapeutic Target", *International Journal of Molecular Science* 22, no. 15 (August

2021), 8220: https://www.ncbi.nlm.nih.gov/pmc/articles/
PMC8348801/#:~:text=Neuronal%20arborisation%20
is%20a%20process,commonly%20reported%20in%20
neurodevelopmental%20disorders. Urbanska et al.
similarly note that "abnormalities in dendritic tree
development lead to serious dysfunction of neuronal
circuits and, consequently, the whole nervous system".

6 Vaishali A. Kulkarni and Bonnie L. Firestein, "The
Dendritic Tree and Brain Disorders", *Molecular and
Cellular Neuroscience* 50, no. 1 (May 2012): 10–20.
https://www.sciencedirect.com/science/article/pii/
S1044743112000450

7 See Goikolea-Vives and Stolp, "Connecting the
Neurobiology of Developmental Brain Injury",
Figure 1: https://pmc.ncbi.nlm.nih.gov/articles/
PMC8348801/#:~:text=Neuronal%20arborisation%20
is%20a%20process,commonly%20reported%20in%20
neurodevelopmental%20disorders

References

Dharani, Krishnagopal. *The Biology of Thought:
A Neuronal Mechanism in the Generation of Thought.*
Cambridge, MA: Academic Press. 2014.

Goikolea-Vives, Ane, and Helen B. Stolp. "Connecting
the Neurobiology of Developmental Brain Injury:
Neuronal Arborisation as a Regulator of Dysfunction
and Potential Therapeutic Target." *International
Journal of Molecular Science* 22, no. 15 (August
2021). https://www.ncbi.nlm.nih.gov/pmc/articles/
PMC8348801/#:~:text=Neuronal%20arborisation%20

is%20a%20process,commonly%20reported%20in%20
neurodevelopmental%20disorders

Kulkarni, Vaishali A., and Bonnie L. Firestein. "The
Dendritic Tree and Brain Disorders." *Molecular and
Cellular Neuroscience* 50, no. 1 (May 2012): 10–20.
https://www.sciencedirect.com/science/article/pii/
S1044743112000450

Urbanska, Malgorzata, Magdalena Blazejczyk, and Jacek
Jaworski. "Molecular Basis of Dendritic Arborization."
ACTA Neurobiologiae Experimentalis 68 (2008): 264–
288. https://ane.pl/index.php/ane/article/view/1695/1695

Chapter 26: Snowflakes Are Miniature "Star Trees"

Geological, Neuronal, and Stellar Dendrites

In the natural world, dendrites are found not only in trees and in nerve cells, but also in the crystalline formations of rocks and snowflakes.

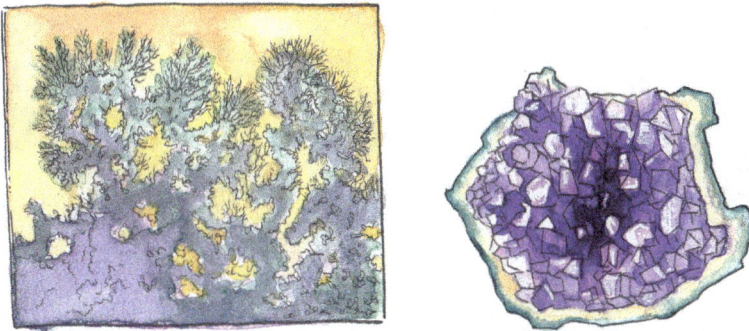

Figure 26.1

DOI: 10.4324/9781003626725-29

Transformation Under Pressure

According to the *Oxford English Dictionary*, dendrites are "crystalline growth[s] of branching or arborescent form" that appear "like a tree or moss" on the surfaces of stones and minerals.[1] Within the field of geology, the term arborization refers to "the production of a tree-like appearance" through "the aggregation of crystals" on the surfaces of rocks. In the watercolor at the beginning of this chapter, a dendritic limestone appears next to an amethyst geode. Despite their differences, both rocks display intricate clusters of crystals on their surfaces, and both have solid stone at their base. The rocks are both grounding and delicate at the same time. They are intriguing examples of transformation under pressure.

Dendritic limestones are sedimentary rocks. This means that they are produced over long periods of time, as layers of deposited earth accumulate, and elements such as iron and manganese oxide crystalize to form delicate branching patterns. Geologists tell us that

> a dendritic pattern often is left within bedding planes of sedimentary rock like shale, limestone, or travertine. The mineral creating the dendritic pattern may be a manganese oxide left behind when water rich in manganese and iron flowed between bedding planes.[2]

Dendritic patterns are created when "a fluid bearing manganese in solution is seeping along a bedding plane surface as little tendrils of liquid". As the liquid dries out, dendritic patterns form on the rock's surface.[3] The distinctive branching patterns can appear in shades of dark purple or deep green. They often resemble botanical forms, such as clusters of branches or mosses. Sometimes the entire surface of a rock can appear like a miniature landscape, or like an enlarged view of the tiny structures one would see under a microscope. A single stone can evoke both the macrocosm and the microcosm.

Just as iron and manganese oxide create deep, rich purple dendritic patterns in sedimentary rocks, these same elements are also found in amethysts.[4] While limestone is a sedimentary rock, amethyst is an igneous rock. This means that the stone was formed through fire and the hardening of molten rock. Amethysts have rich metaphorical associations. While people may think of purple as a lofty color that is associated with royalty, deep violet can also be very grounding. In amethysts, clusters of individual crystals grow out of a solid stone base. Some people find this type of groundedness to be very steadying. Looking at a cluster of amethyst crystals embedded in an underlying matrix of solid stone can serve as a visual metaphor for consolidating one's own thoughts, clearing and calming the mind, and letting go of all the little scattered noises of the day.

Both amethysts and limestones are examples of creativity under pressure, and of the tremendous capacity for transformation. These rocks are literally millions of years old. They are geology—and they are also antiquity. They were formed as the earth created through heat, pressure, and freezing. Just as the rocks are the geological creations of the earth, you also have the power of transformation, of taking the pressures of life to use your intention and create something new.

Miniature Star Trees

Some snowflakes are called stellar dendrites. Literally, these ice crystals are miniature "star trees". As the snowflakes form, multiple symmetrical branches appear within the structure of the crystal. As scientists tell us, "Stellar dendrites have six symmetrical main branches and a large number of randomly placed sidebranches".[5] While all stellar dendrites share the same overall structure, each snowflake is unique, and each is beautiful.[6]

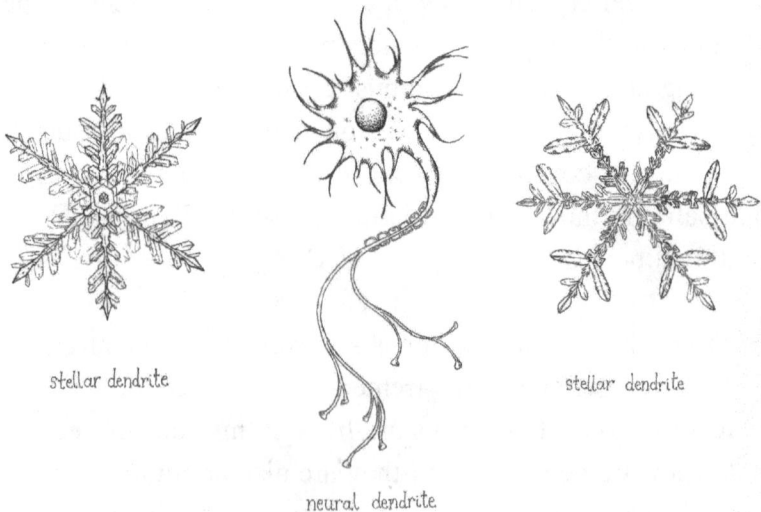

stellar dendrite

neural dendrite

stellar dendrite

Figure 26.2

This calligraphic drawing presents a close-up view of two stellar dendrites flanked by a neural dendrite. As we have seen, in anatomy, dendrites are "any of one or more processes from a nerve cell which are typically short and extensively branched and which conduct impulses toward the cell body".[7] Dendrites can be organic, as in nerve cells and trees, and they can be inorganic, as in rocks and snowflakes. This illustration shows the remarkable similarities between various dendritic structures. The image is at once scientifically accurate, intricately detailed, and absolutely mind-blowing. While the artwork allows you to see how dendrites appear on the micro level, in the next chapter we will approach these subjects on the macro level. We will consider how dendrites provide a striking visual metaphor to envision living in an illuminated world.

Exercise for Reflection and Journaling

As you study the images in this chapter, you can visualize resonant dendritic structures within your own mind and body, and in the world all around you.

- Call up images of dendritic limestones and amethyst crystals online. If possible, study examples of these stones in nature or in a museum. From different perspectives, observe the ways in which the delicate crystals sit atop a base of solid rock. Why is it powerful to reflect on such examples of delicacy *and* groundedness? How do these rocks exemplify the theme of creativity under pressure? How do they enable you to approach a subject from multiple perspectives at once? How might these concepts be useful to you, both analytically and metaphorically? Record your observations in your journal.

- Now look closely at the comparative illustration of the neuronal and stellar dendrites appearing in this chapter. What do these structures have in common and how are they different? Record your reflections in your journal.

- Recognizing the shared dendritic structures of trees, rocks, snowflakes, and neurons represents an exercise in creative analogical thinking. Analogical thinking reflects the ability to identify resonant concepts and images that are situated both within and between various domains of knowledge. As we have seen, visual metaphors and creative analogies can generate a pleasurable response in the brain's limbic system. Now that you have engaged these subjects from complementary perspectives, consider *why* it is both intriguing and powerful to experience such analytical acuity *and* such creative flexibility at the same time. How does this dynamic perspective expand your own thinking while allowing you to be in multiple places at once?

Notes

1 See the entry on "dendrite" in the *OED*: https://www.oed.com/dictionary/dendrite_n?tab=meaning_and_use#7113323

2 Jim Brace-Thompson, "Weird Words: Dendritic", *Rock & Gem* (May 31, 2021): https://www.rockngem.com/weird-words-dendritic/

3 William S. Cordua, "How Do Dendrites Form?"
   (University of Wisconsin-River Falls, 2008): https://
   minds.wisconsin.edu/bitstream/handle/1793/34662/
   Dendrites.pdf?sequence=1
4 According to the *Encyclopaedia Britannica*, an
   amethyst's "physical properties are those of quartz, but
   it contains more iron oxide than any other variety of
   quartz, and experts believe that its colour arises from
   its iron content. Other theories attribute the colour to
   contained manganese or hydrocarbons". See the entry on
   "Amethyst: Mineral" in the *Encyclopaedia Britannica*:
   https://www.britannica.com/science/amethyst
5 Regarding the formal structures of snowflakes, scientists
   note that "although they have complex shapes, each
   stellar dendrite is a single crystal of ice. The molecular
   ordering of the water molecules is the same from one
   side of the crystal to the other". See "Basic Snowflake
   Forms": https://www.nasa.gov/pdf/183517main_
   snowcrystals.pdf. See also "Guide to Snowflakes": http://
   www.snowcrystals.com/guide/guide.html
6 The BBC has noted: "Because a snowflake's shape
   evolves as it journeys through the air, no two will ever be
   the same. Even two flakes floating side by side will each
   be blown through different levels of humidity and vapor
   to create a shape that is truly unique". See BBC Bitesize,
   "Why Are All Snowflakes Unique?": https://www.bbc.
   co.uk/bitesize/articles/zmqmrj6#:~:text=Because%20
   a%20snowflake's%20shape%20evolves,shape%20that%20
   is%20truly%20unique
7 See the entry on "dendrite" in the *OED*: https://www.oed.
   com/dictionary/dendrite_n?tab=meaning_and_use#7113323

References

"Amethyst: Mineral." *Encyclopaedia Britannica*. https://www.britannica.com/science/amethyst

"Basic Snowflake Forms." https://www.nasa.gov/pdf/183517main_snowcrystals.pdf

BBC Bitesize. "Why Are All Snowflakes Unique?" https://www.bbc.co.uk/bitesize/articles/zmqmrj6#:~:text=Because%20a%20snowflake's%20shape%20evolves,shape%20that%20is%20truly%20unique.

Brace-Thompson, Jim. "Weird Words: Dendritic." *Rock & Gem.* May 31, 2021. https://www.rockngem.com/weird-words-dendritic/

Cordua, William S. "How Do Dendrites Form?" University of Wisconsin-River Falls, 2008. https://minds.wisconsin.edu/bitstream/handle/1793/34662/Dendrites.pdf?sequence=1

"Guide to Snowflakes." http://www.snowcrystals.com/guide/guide.html

Simpson, J.A., and E.S.C. Weiner, eds. *The Oxford English Dictionary*. 2nd ed. Oxford: Clarendon Press. 1989.

Chapter 27: As Snow Falls in the Forest, Light Shines in the Mansion

Dendritic Connections in an Illuminated World

Much like snow falling steadily in the forest, intricate patterns of connection and communication unfold in the world all around us, and they are generated and regenerated, in every living moment.

Figure 27.1

DOI: 10.4324/9781003626725-30

Throughout this book, we have approached dendritic structures on the micro level, through neurons, trees, rocks, and snowflakes. Now we're going to step back and approach these structures on the macro level by considering the visual metaphor of snow falling in the forest surrounding the mansion of the brain.

Throughout the natural world,
Dendrites reflect the patterns of creation:
How it forms,
How it communicates,
And how it networks.
This can be seen in human interactions, as well.
When you see a person walking down the street,
And you exchange gazes,
You can imagine this as the equivalent
Of dendrites reaching out and touching one another,
To gather and process information intuitively.

The message could be: "Oh, don't go that way.
Go this way.
This way is nicer.
This way is easier".
Information is always moving in and out,
And adjustments are always being made,
To meet whatever is coming.
The seemingly empty space all around us
Is filled with subtle structures of communication
That form an interconnected field.

Dendrites are part of a vast web of communication and connection.

This is a highly dynamic space.
It is a space of creation.
The connections can be seen and felt in the earth and in
the air,
And in all of life communicating together.
The dendritic connections are in the water droplets of the
snowflakes.
They are in the birds in the tree branches,
They are in the leaves and roots of the trees,
And they are in the nerve cells of your own brain and body,
All of which are in communication
All the time.

The connections are in everything.
They are in us,
And they are all around us,
And they are generated and regenerated
In every living moment.

Patterns of Connection and Creation

The vast number of connections that we experience every
single day—while just walking around, living our lives—
is absolutely spectacular. The connections occur every
moment, in every breath, in order to sustain our bodies
and give us a home to live in. Because the patterns are
so vast, they can be very difficult to conceptualize. The
artworks appearing in this chapter provide intriguing ways
to envision such a complex interconnected world.

In the opening watercolor, newly fallen snow settles
in the tree limbs and branches surrounding the stately

mansion. As we saw in Chapter 5, the mansion serves as a visual metaphor for the brain as a majestic form of wired architecture. The arcing patterns of golden light appearing in the mansion's windows resemble the peaking form of an action potential. An action potential is a graphic representation of the rapid rise and fall of electricity as it passes across a cell membrane. When a person is in a state of focused attention and inspiration, their synapses fire. Cellular pathways link up to form connections, and their brain lights up. As we saw in Chapter 8, all thought patterns leave a neuronal trail, which can be visualized metaphorically as deer trails through the woods. The artworks appearing in this chapter provide striking

Figure 27.2

metaphors to envision the networked structures that run through an interconnected brain *and* through an illuminated world.

When a person does not feel connected to their world,
Things can become extremely difficult for them.
When a person is feeling anxious or lost or lonely,
It can feel like the rooms in the mansion are all dark,
Except for maybe just one.
Then the brain is not lit up.
Connections are a gift because,
Without them, the world would be a much darker place,
in every way.
Connections light connections,
In the brain and in the world.

A Field of Open Possibilities

Just as synaptic connections are formed in the tiny spaces between neurons, these spaces are like open fields of possibility that hold the potential for connection and communication. They are like the blank areas of a black and white drawing, which are just waiting to be filled in. When this occurs, the world appears in a different light.

In the next image, the same landscape appears in vibrant shades of deep pine green, pale shimmering indigo, and warm glowing gold—all of which are surrounded by scattered flashes of silver and white. The grace of the falling snow is a metaphor for an epiphany—a moment of

Figure 27.3

powerful inspiration and realization. Just as the individual snowflakes resemble falling stars (or stellar dendrites), they offer a creative visual metaphor for the type of illumination that can fall quickly into your mind, wash through your thoughts, and light a fire within you so that you can look at the world in a different light.

When we feel inspired,
It may feel like a breath of fresh air is moving through us.
It may feel like effervescent sparks of silver and gold
Are flashing in our brain.
These little sparks are both luminous and reflective.
They are like the snowflakes falling through the sky,
Falling through the light,
And dancing in the wind.[1]

Exercise for Reflection and Journaling

The images featured in this chapter show how living webs of connection and communication are woven throughout our bodies and throughout the natural world.

- After looking at the snow scenes appearing in this chapter, go back and look at the various illustrations of the illuminated brain appearing in Part One of the book. What do these images have in common? How do you feel when you look at them? What parts of your own brain approach these subjects intellectually and analytically? What parts of your brain approach these subjects creatively and artistically? How do you feel when you consciously recognize the patterns of connection and communication that thread through your thinking? How does it feel to know that you are standing in multiple places at once, in your mind and in your brain?

- Now go back and compare the different artistic styles of the two landscapes appearing in this chapter. The first image is loosely abstracted, while the second is more precise and linear. The artworks evoke comparative visions of the same subject. Which artistic style do you prefer and why? What would be lost if only one style appeared, and not the other? There are no right or wrong answers to these questions. Reflecting on these themes provides a mirror of your own thoughts and a complementary way for you to approach your own mind.

- Now compare the black and white and the color images of the mansion in the forest. How are the two scenes similar and how are they different? Once again, you can approach the black and white drawing as part of an adult coloring book. You can make copies of the image and experiment with various harmonious and disharmonious color combinations and note your responses in your journal.

- How is engaging with these themes all part of the art of transformation?

Note

1 The last lines of the poem are taken from my book *The Colors of Life: Exploring Life Experience Through Color and Emotion* (New York: Routledge, 2025), 108.

References

Brennan, Marcia. *The Colors of Life: Exploring Life Experience Through Color and Emotion.* New York: Routledge. 2025.

Chapter 28: The Mirror Transforms

Living Between Memory and Epiphany

Our inner and our outer worlds can be like mirrors of one another.

The Psyche as the Mirror and as the Mind

When I write about the color yellow in my book *The Colors of Life*, I invite readers to imagine that they have a mirror inside of themselves:

The color yellow is like an inner mirror of self-awareness and self-reflection. Deep in the pit of your stomach, in your own gut, you know how you truly feel about things, and you constantly reflect these feelings back to yourself. Yellow is the inner sense of self-awareness that sits at your very center. Yellow reflects how you really feel, and not what the external world projects onto you or tells you about what you want and how you should be feeling. Yellow is like a mirror that reflects what is going on deep inside yourself, at your very center.[1]

DOI: 10.4324/9781003626725-31

Figure 28.1

The word "psyche", which lies at the root of the word "psychology", resonates with these themes. The term means mirror, as well as mind, soul, and consciousness.[2] When we recognize how our thoughts and emotions can become reflected in the world around us, we can create more space for insight, wisdom, vision, and reflection.

Mending Broken Shards

In Chapter 21, an ornate mirror in a golden frame hangs in the magical bathroom inside the mansion of the brain. The bathroom is a space for cleansing, renewal, self-care, and self-reflection. Now the same mirror appears as a metaphor for brokenness *and* for wholeness. In the image appearing in this chapter, a person gazes at a cracked mirror, in which shards of glass seem to be flying out at the corners. Yet instead of the glass flying outward, the shards are actually flying inward, as though a film were being run in reverse. As the broken mirror mends before the person's eyes, crystalline flashes of silver and gold evoke sparkles of insight and illumination.

When a person with anxiety or OCD begins to worry about a thousand things at once, it's as if they shatter in a thousand different directions. If a person shatters, then they want to collapse. But if the process can be recognized as it begins, it can be interrupted. Then the person has a moment to re-center themselves, to take a deep breath, to ask for assistance, and to move toward a more solid place in their own mind. This can be visualized metaphorically. Imagine yourself standing before a shattered mirror and watching the glass fly—not outward in all directions—but inward, toward the center. As you do this, you can imagine the mirror mending inside of yourself.

The snow scenes discussed in the previous chapter provide complementary ways to visualize the themes of unity and fragmentation. As snow falls in the forest surrounding the mansion of the brain, the flying fragments of the individual snowflakes create a unified scene. This is not a landscape of brokenness, but a complex vision of an interconnected world.

A Gentle Play Between the Old and the New

As you practice working with these metaphors, you may begin to look at life differently, including at your past and at what lies ahead of you. As you do this, you may be wondering where in the brain our memories are held, and where we contemplate the subjects of transformation and transcendence. As discussed in Part One, these responses occur in different locations in the brain. When we contemplate a memory, we may be engaging the hypothalamus and the thalamus. When we contemplate an epiphany, it may feel like energies are pouring through the frontal cortex and the pituitary gland into the conscious mind. As you consider these subjects, you can contemplate an interplay of the old and the new:

The play of the old and the new is like a ping pong game.
This book can help you to approach these subjects
In a new light,

So that you can play a nice easy game
Between the old and the new.
A nice easy game
Between memory and epiphany.

Exercise for Reflection and Journaling

- In a quiet moment, practice the visualization of the mending mirror. Close your eyes and clear your thoughts. In your mind's eye, picture a shattered mirror hanging on a wall in front of you. Instead of seeing the shards of glass flying outward, imagine the fragments coming back together, as though you were watching a film in reverse. Practice this exercise a few times and then open your eyes. What did you learn? How do you feel? Why might it be useful to practice this self-reflective exercise before you actually find yourself in a shattering experience? Record your thoughts in your journal.
- If you have a memory that you don't like, you can always close your eyes and ask to have more detachment from that memory. You can picture the psychic residue of the memory as being like streaks on a mirror. As you request detachment, you can imagine your own hand wiping the mirror with a damp cloth so that the glass is clean and the surface shines brightly again.

Notes

1 Marcia Brennan, *The Colors of Life: Exploring Life Experience Through Color and Emotion* (New York: Routledge, 2025), 106.

2 See the definition of "psyche" in the *OED*: https://
   www.oed.com/dictionary/psyche_n?tab=meaning_and_
   use&hide-all-quotations=true#27724240

References

Brennan, Marcia. *The Colors of Life: Exploring Life
   Experience Through Color and Emotion.* New York:
   Routledge. 2025.
Simpson, J.A., and E.S.C. Weiner, eds. *The Oxford English
   Dictionary.* 2nd ed. Oxford: Clarendon Press. 1989.

Chapter 29: Return to the Magical Classroom

Neuroaesthetics and the Art of Transformation

Welcome back! That was quite an exploration, wasn't it?

Figure 29.1

DOI: 10.4324/9781003626725-32

Going Beyond Where We Started

As you can see, we are now sitting in the same place where the story began. There is the same microscope, the same model of the human brain, the same colorful fMRI imagery, the same books on the shelves, the same enlarged snowflake, and the same teapot and philodendrons. Yet you may now be looking at these subjects in a new light. Take a moment to collect your thoughts and observe what has changed inside of you. While everything in the classroom looks the same, the lesson is now at an end and the seasons have shifted. Instead of morning sunlight streaming in through the windows and soft green leaves appearing on the trees outside, snow is falling from the sky and, even though you can't see it, the lights of the mansion are twinkling gently in the distance.

The tonal keynotes of this image are warm brown, emerald green, and silver-white. These colors unite the groundedness of the earth with the transformational processes of growth and illumination. When I teach and when I write, I also think of the color gold. Gold evokes the synapses that fire in the brain and that light the mind. At its heart, teaching is the art of illumination and transformation, and this knowledge is both anointed and appointed with gold.

Accessing Your Own Inner Gold

You can always access your own inner knowing, your own inner gold. You can always step back to gain sufficient distance from a subject to observe what is unfolding. From the moment that you were born, you have had a clear and open pathway for receiving such information. As you go through life, the pathway can become a bit clogged. You can picture this as being like a funnel with some goop in it. The funnel is always there, and the opening is always possible, but from time to time, you have to clean out the goop with a funnel brush. Think of your own learning process as equivalent to running your own little scientific experiments, with the goals of cleansing and expansion, growth and transformation. You don't have to do everything perfectly, or all at once. Just stay with the inquiry, make careful notes, and be conscious of your own processes of transformation.

Throughout this book, there is a sense of invitation.
It's as though I'm saying:
Come and experience something new.
See life from a different perspective—
Even, your connection to your own brain,
Your brain's connection to how you feel,
Your own ability to change and maneuver,
Your relationship to color, art, language, science, and to the world itself.
This book is an invitation to see something new.
Especially—yourself.

There will be times when forgiveness, compassion, and gratitude are all parts of the experiment. Some days you will just have to say:

I forgive myself for the difficult thoughts and behaviors that arose today. I recognize my own willingness to look at these challenging things, and to see them clearly. I also recognize that it takes a lot of energy and courage to do this type of work. I thank myself for showing myself what is really there, *especially* when it is difficult to look at. And now that I've looked at some difficult things, how can I make all of this easier? How can I make this more beautiful?

In the first chapter of this book, I told you that the field of neuroaesthetics concerns the application of the science of the brain to the study of art. Now that you have reached the end, you can see how the structures of the human brain and its patterns of thought can *themselves* provide the bases for an innovative conceptual artwork, and how this type of creative analogical thinking can help you to shape your own psychic landscape. As you practice these skills, you gain valuable insight into your own processes of worldbuilding. And then, you can go and write your own neurocognitive fairytales and, most importantly, be the author of your own stories.

Exercise for Reflection and Journaling

Just as the field of neuroaesthetics draws on the insights of the arts, the sciences, and the humanities, there are many different types of classrooms and many different tools of learning.

- If you were to design your own magical classroom, what would it look like? What learning tools would appear in your classroom and why would they be needed? What kind of emotional tone would you use to establish the culture of your classroom? What kinds of classes would you design and teach, and what would you want your students to learn?

- What have you learned about the relationships between the arts, the sciences, and the humanities? How might you imagine bringing these fields together in novel ways to build new worlds and to tell new stories?
- How does exploring these concepts help you to be in multiple places at once? How is this all part of the art of transformation?

Chapter 30: The Living Map

Deer Trails Through the Woods

Figure 30.1

Have you ever seen a deer trail through the woods?
If you were walking,
And you were to come up above the woods,
Up above the forest,
You would see many wonderful, beautiful, natural trails

DOI: 10.4324/9781003626725-33

Made by the animals whose tracks are interlinking,
Intertwining,
Taking them to all their natural resources,
To places they need to go,
For rest,
For food,
For water,
For community.
This would all be in a lush green forest,
With deep brown earth,
And wherever you turn,
Wherever you look,
The pathways are very beautiful.

Both Intimate and Expansive

This woodland scene is both intimate and expansive, intricate and panoramic. Beneath the lush green canopy of the forest, deer and rabbits stand beside a flowing stream. The distant branches of the water and the crisscrossing limbs of the overhead trees are all dendritic. The fallen tree trunk in the foreground provides an ideal place to sit and contemplate this striking metaphorical imagery. Notice how the landscape is at once grounded and elevated, naturalistic and visionary. As you enter such a world, you are standing in multiple places at once.

As you contemplate the scene, you also realize that you are no longer standing in the same place as you were when the story began. Because you now understand so much more, you can envision a more expansive set of connections and

Figure 30.2

possibilities. Looking at the opening and closing landscapes together provides a way for you to see how far you have come. Now you can view these subjects in a different light, to align your inner and outer vision and to approach the world in a new way.

Going Where the Pathways Light Up

Being in alignment means that,
When you turn your head to the right,
You consciously notice that the path does not light up.
But when you turn your head to the left,

Your orbitofrontal cortex lights up,
And you say to yourself, "I'm going that way!"
Your internal awareness tells you:
Take ten steps, turn right, then turn left.
You keep going where the pathway lights up.

You are following your own path of alignment.
You are not endlessly repeating what you have already
learned,
And what you already know.
Anxiety and OCD are really lessons in alignment,
Or in the lack of alignment.
Now you are learning how to trust yourself.
You are learning how to follow the path that feels
All lit up inside of you.

Here's the epiphany:
*The pathways are **alive.***
Whether they are of deer trails through the woods,
Or the neural pathways of your own brain,
They are all made up of living energies.

This book is like a roadmap for exploring these living
pathways.
The pathways are alive,
And the connections are in everything.
They are in you, and they are all around you,
And they are generated and regenerated,
In every living moment.

Exercise for Reflection and Journaling

- As you look carefully at the opening and closing images of deer trails through the woods, take a moment to consider what has changed in your thinking. Are you standing in the same place as you were when the book began? What has shifted in you, and how do you envision a new path forward?

Index

Note: Page numbers in *italics* indicate a figure, and page numbers followed by an "n" indicate a note on the corresponding page.